A manual of modern rope techniques

A manual of modern rope techniques

for climbers and mountaineers

Nigel Shepherd

Constable London

First published in Great Britain 1990
by Constable & Company Limited
3 The Lanchesters, 162 Fulham Palace Road
London W6 9ER
Copyright © 1990 by Nigel Shepherd
Reprinted 1992, 1993, 1995, 1996, 1997
ISBN 0 09 469170 3
Printed in Great Britain by
BAS Printers Ltd, Over Wallop, Hampshire

A CIP catalogue record for this book
is available from the British Library

Contents

List of Illustrations

8

NOTES ON PHOTOGRAPHY

All the technical photographs have been set up to illustrate a particular technique in the simplest way possible. Inevitably, this has meant that some illustrations do not appear to be to scale. I trust that the reader will understand this concession to clarity.

All photographs are by the author.

12

A garland twined from varied
waifs and strays

The flowers of thoughtless
youth and later days.

T. C. S. Corry
Irish Lyrics, Songs and Poems 1879

Acknowledgements

No book of this kind can ever be entirely the work of one person. It must, by its very nature, be a medley of many people's experiences.

To this end I am indebted to lots of people – climbing partners of old and new, novice to superstar – for sharing their experiences and some great days out in the mountains.

In putting this book together I owe a particular debt and I wish to record my thanks.

To Sir Charles Evans for kind permission to quote from his fine book *On Climbing*, still an inspirational instruction book 30 years on. To Martin Atkinson and Mammut for being so generous in supplying equipment for the photographs. To Billy Wayman for some of the best climbing days ever and sharing his extensive technical knowledge. To Brian Hall for reading the manuscript. To Louisa Stieger for helping with the action photos. To Jules and Barbara and Michel at Sport Extreme in Chamonix for the loan of equipment.,

Finally to Helen for lots of things too numerous to mention but mostly for just being there.

This book is for them. Any credit due we shall share but any criticism is entirely my responsibility.

Nigel Shepherd
Chamonix, August 1989

Introduction

This book is the successor to *Self Rescue Techniques for Climbers and Instructors* (Adventure Unlimited, 1987) which grew from a frustration at the lack of information and the myths surrounding self rescue. This new volume is the result of a job half done. It is not meant to supersede all that has been written before; neither is it intended to be the definitive tome on a wide and essentially varied theme. I do hope, however, that it is thought-provoking and I also hope that in some ways it is contradictory to more established practices. This is a technical manual and should, I believe, encourage thought, discussion and criticism among those who read it.

Throughout the narrative I have assumed that I am talking to climbers and mountaineers who are reasonably competent at handling themselves on crag and mountain, both in terms of climbing ability and technical ropework. Anyone basically, who can tie on to a rope and belay safely and effectively.

I am aware that much more could have been said about some of the techniques and the possible variations. If the text is lacking in this respect it is because I felt further information would unnecessarily complicate the book and that readers should be allowed an element of self-discovery – the most valuable of all learning processes. Neither do I wish to be dogmatic in my presentation of techniques. I am well aware that there are other ways of doing things that are equally acceptable and that so also are there people with different ideas.

I have tried to keep everything as realistic as possible in that no extra equipment is used other than that which is normally carried. Whilst I do mention a few bits of specialized equipment, there are few things that couldn't be done with normal day to day climbing gear.

Many of the techniques shown and described in this book

require a good deal of practice before putting them to the test in a 'real situation'. You would be well advised to choose your practice areas carefully. A site with good anchor points, a steepish slab and flat ground below would be ideal. Never work high above the ground until you feel confident at performing a particular task.

Finally, I would welcome any comments that readers may have, critical or otherwise.

Good and safe climbing.

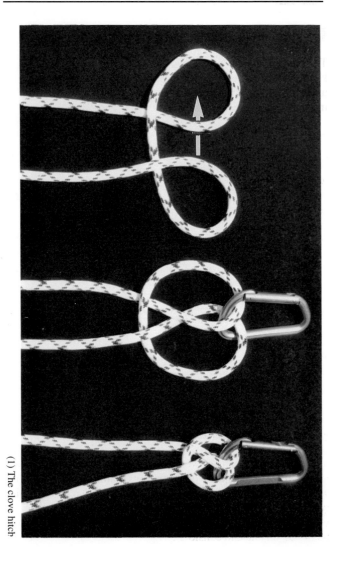

(1) The clove hitch

Useful Knots and Basic Techniques

This section of the book covers all sorts of basic techniques, knots and methods of tying on to the rope that will be found useful in day to day climbing and mountaineering, and also in the more problematical rescue and self help situations.

In dealing with individual knots or techniques I have treated each in isolation and then made suggestions as to where they might fit in best in the overall rope safety system. By practising each one thoroughly as a separate entity the reader should be able to identify and integrate one or a number of the knots or techniques into his or her day to day climbing and any self-help rescue situation.

As with all knots and techniques there are any number of ways of tying them or putting them into operation. The methods described here are fairly simple and straightforward but once you have mastered the basic skills I'm quite sure you will evolve your own methods of arriving at a safe and correct result.

THE KNOTS

Clove Hitch

This knot has been in common usage throughout Europe for a great many years. Its popularity among UK climbers is increasing as people discover its versatility. Form two loops identically as in Photo 1 and pass the right behind the left. With practice the knot can be tied with one hand – useful if you are hanging on for grim death and anxious to arrange an anchor.

There are one or two things that you should be aware of in using this knot. It can be a very difficult knot to undo after it has been subjected to a heavy or continuous loading, particularly in wet ropes or in soft tubular tape. You should also try to avoid tying it in the end of the rope as there may be some slippage. If you do have to tie it in the rope end, make sure that you have plenty of tail end and consider tying off with a couple of hitches or half a double fisherman's (page 25).

Useful applications

For tying in directly to anchor points, but only if they are in arm's reach of your stance (see Tying on to Anchors page 114)

Can be used to bring two anchor points to a single point of attachment with a tape or rope sling (Photo 55a)

Tying off pitons on ice or rock

Securing the rope from an anchor point back to the harness

Tying slings or climbing ropes around anchor stakes

Italian Hitch

A most useful 'sliding friction' knot. Like the clove hitch, it has been in popular usage throughout continental Europe for many years, particularly as a method of safeguarding climbing companions. It is sometimes called a *Munter hitch*.

To tie this knot, form two loops identically, as in the clove hitch and fold the two together as in Photo 2. It is important that the two loops are formed in the same way otherwise the end result may well be a simple two turns around the karabiner. This will not afford any safety whatsoever. It is best used on a large pear-shaped screwgate karabiner.

I have often heard it said that this knot causes nylon to rub over nylon so must be unsafe to use. The nylon over nylon danger arises only in situations where a moving nylon rope runs over a static nylon rope. If you study the Italian hitch carefully whilst it is in use, you will see quite clearly that this is not the case. Nylon has a very low melting point, and it is quite possible in situations where a moving rope runs over a static item of kit such as a harness, to generate enough heat to melt the nylon.

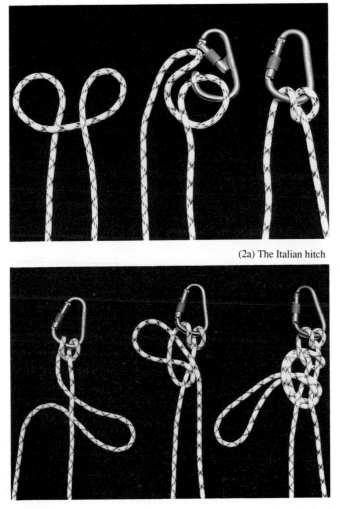

(2a) The Italian hitch

(2b) Tying off an Italian hitch while under load

There are some points to watch out for in use. It twists the rope very badly. Strangely enough some ropes twist more than others, probably due to individual manufacturers' construction designs. This problem can be alleviated to a certain extent by not allowing the rope to twist as it passes through your hand. It is difficult to hold a serious leader fall as the rope slips around the karabiner quite quickly on initial impact. Provided that you can keep a grip on the rope during this early stage a fall is soon arrested. Wearing leather gloves makes it much safer to use. If you are using it as for abseiling on double ropes, it is advisable to treat the two ropes as one and only tie one knot. Using the hitch in narrow karabiners can cause the knot to jam at inconvenient times so it is recommended that you use a large pear-shaped or HMS karabiner. Photo 2b shows how to tie off the hitch under load.

Useful applications

As a lowering, abseiling or belaying device

Can be used on a 'direct belay' (page 177)

Double Fisherman's and Double Fisherman's with Reef Knot

The traditional knot for joining two ends of rope together is the double fisherman's. There is such a thing as a single fisherman's but it is not in common usage nor indeed recommended as it does not have the same holding power. The double fisherman's with reef knot is a good safe knot and is easy to undo after being subjected to a heavy loading, for example when a number of climbers go down the same abseil or when it is necessary to get off the mountain by numerous abseils and the ropes are not untied between each stage. Frequently check the knot for signs of loosening.

When tying the double fisherman's knot you must make

(3) Double fisherman's and double fisherman's with reef knot

(4) The sheet bend

sure that both halves fit snugly into each other. If they don't, the knot is wrong and may come undone when subjected to a severe load (Photo 3).

Whenever you use the knot make sure that there is, at the very least, 4 cm of tail end at each side and that the knot is tied firmly and securely. If you use it to join the ends of rope slung nuts make sure that the knot is well tightened. You should check it frequently for signs of wear and loosening. Do not use it to join two ends of tape together. It is nowhere near as safe or neat as a tape knot.

Useful applications

Joining two ropes together on long abseils

Joining the two ends of a rope slung nut

Half a double fisherman's knot is commonly used for tying off the knot that is used to tie into a harness. This is sometimes referred to as a double stopper knot

Sheet Bend

This knot has very few applications in climbing and mountaineering but is included because it is used in tying the Parisienne baudrier (page 86). It is possible to use it between the double fisherman's knot in place of the reef knot when abseiling. You may also find it useful in self-help situations when you have run out or are short of karabiners. It can be used to connect two slings together but make sure that there is plenty of tail end. It can be used equally well in tape or rope of different diameters but do not mix tape with rope (Photo 4).

Useful applications

Tying the Parisienne baudrier

Used in a double fisherman's knot instead of a reef knot (see page 22)

The Tape Knot or Ring Bend

This is the recommended knot for joining two ends of tape together and is most commonly used for making up slings. It is essentially an overhand knot in one end of the length of tape and the other end retraces the line back through the knot to come out on the opposite side (Photo 5). Unlike the fisherman's knot which shouldn't be used in tape, the tape knot can be used in rope. Make sure that the tape lies flat throughout the whole knot and that there is at least 4 cm of tail end. Frequently check any knots tied in thick or 'super blue' tape for signs of loosening. Some people stitch the ends of the knot down but personally I do not recommend this as I have seen the knot move along the sling but still appear to be tied. If used in rope ensure that all the strands lie parallel throughout the knot (Photo 5).

Useful applications

Joining two ends of tape together to make a sling

Joining two ends of rope together to make a sling

KNOTS FOR TYING ON TO THE ROPE.

The Central Loop

There is a bewildering array of harnesses for climbing available these days. The type of harness that is used most commonly throughout the world is the sit harness – full body harnesses are awkward to handle and constrictive to wear in most mountaineering situations.

    The technology and design of sit harnesses has come a long way since the first purpose-made waist belt of some 25 years ago.

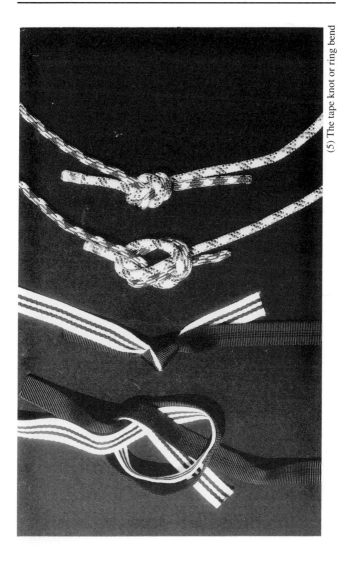

(5) The tape knot or ring bend

All harnesses have specific requirements for tying in to the rope and each individual manufacturer is obliged to provide information on the way in which to tie the rope into a particular harness. You would be well advised to pay close attention to that information as in some cases it may be extremely dangerous to tie in any other way.

In nearly all harnesses there are loops through which the rope should be threaded and these are referred to as the 'tie-on loops'. After threading the rope through these loops a suitable knot is tied to secure the rope to the harness. The loop that is then formed is referred to as the *central loop* and it is crucial to modern rope techniques, particularly those described in this book. Photo 10 shows the loop clearly.

On modern harnesses it plays an important role in attaching belaying devices and for tying on to anchor points. It can also affect the way in which you are able to escape from the system (page 144) and whether or not you are able to do this with your harness intact. The same photo also illustrates how it is used to clip in belay devices and to secure the climber to the anchor point which is, in this case, a clove hitch.

Bowline

This knot and the figure of eight are without a doubt the most commonly used for tying on to the end of the rope. The bowline is the more traditional, having been used since the early days of mountaineering.

It can be tied into all harnesses with equal security. The basic knot is illustrated in Photos 6a and b. It is important to ensure that the knot is finished off with a half a double fisherman's knot for extra security. This should fit snugly up against the bowline. For further security the knot can be tied with the 'rabbit coming out of two holes' (Photo 6c). This also makes the knot easier to undo after being subjected to a shock load. When tying this knot many people use the 'rabbit out of a hole, around the tree and back in the hole again' technique. It is important to

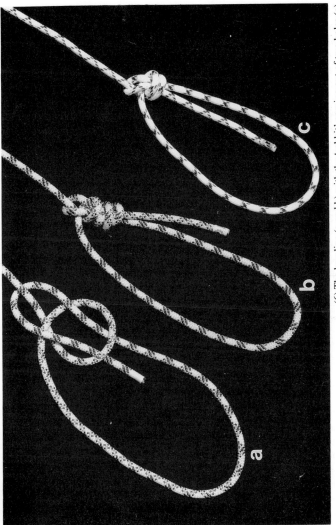

(6) The bowline (a and b) with the 'rabbit' coming out of two holes (c)

ensure that the tree is the main climbing rope in every case.

It can be used to tie the climbing rope directly around the waist. This of course is not as comfortable as a harness but may be necessary from time to time. It will almost certainly cause asphyxiation and death within a short time if you try to hang free with a rope tied directly around the waist.

Useful applications

Tying the end of the rope into the harness

Tying the end of the rope around a tree or block or thread anchor

Tying the rope directly around the waist. Only recommended if no harness is available

There are two variations of the bowline that may also be found useful. The first is the bowline on the bight. Photo 7 shows how to tie this knot. Initially it can be a little frustrating to tie but like all knots once mastered it is rarely forgotten. This can be used for connecting a sit harness to a chest harness (page 88) or for bringing two anchor points into one central point. The second variation is the triple bowline (Photo 8). This is essentially used as an improvised body harness. Don't expect it to provide much comfort however!

It is best tied by wrapping the rope around your waist, doubled of course, and then tying a bowline in the normal way but without the double stopper knot to finish it off. Step out of the loop once it is tied. Three loops are formed in doing this and all should be exactly the same size.

To use it as a harness put a leg through a loop each. The third loop goes over your head and one arm. The knot should be at about sternum level.

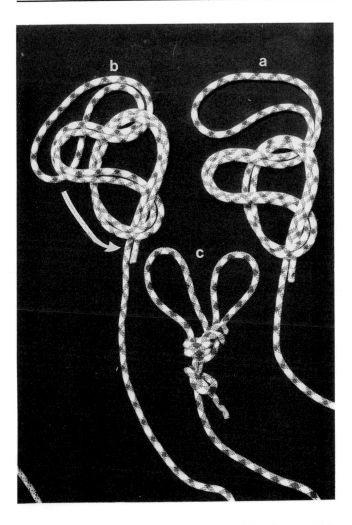

(7) Bowline on the bight

(8) The triple bowline

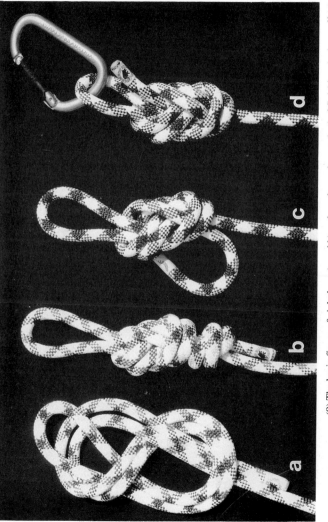

(9) The basic figure of eight knot (a and b) and an alternative method of finishing the knot off (c)

The Figure of Eight

This is the other commonly used knot but is slightly more versatile than the bowline as it can be tied in a number of different ways. In its simplest form the figure of eight is tied in a bight of the rope and the finished product provides a loop which can be clipped into a karabiner. This is useful for top-roping or safety-roping situations where the rope is clipped into the harness with a screwgate krab but is generally an inconvenient way of tying in to most harnesses (Photo 9).

There is actually very little that can go wrong when tying the figure of eight but people sometimes end up with an overhand knot or a figure of sixteen or even thirty-two! These are all adequate although the overhand is difficult to undo after loading and the others are just plain cumbersome. A second useful application is for tying in to a harness directly through the manufacturer's recommended tie in loops. Be sure to familiarize yourself with each individual harness tie in method.

When tying the knot directly into the harness the first step is to tie a figure of eight knot in the single rope about 60 cm from the end. The end is then threaded through the tie in loops and the knot completed by tracing the end back through the single figure of eight. Be sure that the ropes going through the knot lie parallel and that the finished loop is neither too small or too large. As a guide to the correct size you should just be able to get your fist through the loop (Photo 10).

The figure of eight can also be used to tie into the middle of the rope. It is not ideal for this purpose – an Alpine butterfly (page 39) is better – but it does suffice. It is tied in a bight of the rope and the loop that is formed can be clipped into a karabiner in the harness. (See Tying into the Middle of the Rope page 184.)

As with the bowline and any other knot in the end of a rope, you should always finish off with the double stopper knot or half a double fisherman's. In most cases this contributes negligibly to the strength of the knot but an enormous amount to the safety of the knot for it ensures that there is enough tail end of rope to

(10) Tying the end of the rope into the harness with a figure of eight knot

(11) Figure of eight on the bight

absorb shock without the rope pulling through the knot.

Photo 9c and d shows an alternative way of finishing off the figure of eight knot by tucking the end back into the knot. It is quite popular and uses less rope than a double stopper knot.

Another way in which the figure of eight can be used is in tying back to the harness from an anchor point. This is done using the knot tied in a bight of rope or by threading the doubled rope through the central loop and securing it with a somewhat unwieldy but nevertheless effective knot (see page 115 and Photo 51a). You should be aware that this method is only safe if tied around something of a small diameter, such as illustrated here, the central loop. It would not for instance be as safe to tie it around the harness belt.

The figure of eight, like the bowline, can be tied 'on the bight' that is to say the finished product forms a double loop (Photo 11). This has few applications in climbing other than those already mentioned on page 30 when discussing the bowline on the bight.

Useful applications

Tying into the end of rope

Tying back to the harness from an anchor point

Tying in to the middle of the rope

The Three-Quarters Fisherman

This knot is only included because it is a rather neat way of tying in to the rope end. It is rarely, if ever, used in the UK and the only places I have ever seen it used are the USA and New Zealand. As an addition to your repertoire, however, it is interesting to know and perhaps try.

To begin with you tie an overhand in the single rope about 45 cm from the end. Thread the end through the tie in loops and

(12) The three–quarters fisherman's

then pass it through the single knot, finishing off with a double stopper knot or half a double fisherman's (Photo 12).

Useful applications

Tying in to rope end

The Alpine Butterfly

This knot is used for tying into the middle of the rope. It is by far the most suitable knot to use in this situation as it does not put any undue twisting or distorting action on the knot in the event of being subjected to a load. Indeed, it could be said that the knot is designed purely for this purpose.

Although not in common usage, this knot is gaining credence and popularity. I suspect that one of the reasons it has been so ignored over the years is that it is quite complicated to tie (Photos 13a to f). When tying into the middle of the rope one can clip in directly to the loop with a screwgate karabiner. One of the problems, however, with being tied in to the middle of the rope when moving together (page 178) is that one is constantly being pulled from in front or held back from behind. This is particularly awkward for any 'middle people' as they may be on a tricky section of climbing just as the rope becomes tight. Similarly if one member of the party slips there is a chance that they may take the rest with them.

A way around these problems is to tie an Alpine butterfly knot in the rope with a long attachment loop. In the end of the loop you can then tie a figure of eight knot and clip this into your harness. The length of the attachment from harness to Alpine butterfly should be no longer than arm's reach for safety (Photo 14).

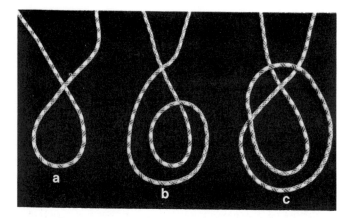

(13) Tying…

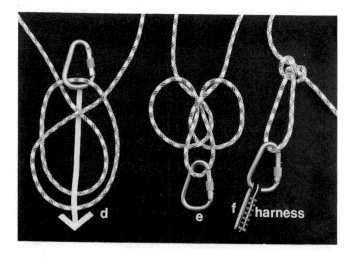

…and finishing off the Alpine butterfly

(14) Attachment to the middle of the rope

(15) The figure of eight with half fisherman's

The Figure of Eight with Half Fisherman's

Photo 15 clearly shows how this knot is used. A particularly useful application of this knot is in situations where you have a few people to rope up a short section of climbing, on a scramble for instance, and you don't trust the members of your party to tie their own knots correctly.

Tie a figure of eight knot in the single rope then tie a half double fisherman's beyond it. You must make sure that the half fisherman's is finished with the end of rope pointing away from the figure of eight. It is often easier to tie the knot around your own waist first. Once tied, step out of it by sliding the half fisherman's knot away from you. The single figure of eight remains in position. To fit the loop to a smaller person all that is needed is to move the figure of eight away from the half fisherman's. To fit a fatter person move it towards the half fisherman's. When the person steps into the loop, it is a simple matter to tighten it by sliding the two knots together. The two knots must butt up against each other so that when tied around the waist they form a snug but not overly tight or slack loop.

PRUSIK KNOTS

I use the collective term 'prusik knots' because it is the generally accepted term to describe knots that can be used to ascend a fixed rope – or to descend for that matter. They are also used in self-rescue situations to temporarily secure a rope and some can be used as safety back-up devices or autoblocs (see page 48).

All of the knots described, apart from the Penberthy knot, require a sling of 5 mm or 6 mm cord joined together with a double fisherman's or ring bend. The Penberthy can be used with rope or cord of any diameter provided that the rope that you are tying it to is 9 mm or thicker. It does not require a closed loop though (page 50). Some of them can be tied with tape slings. For information on the length of loops refer to the section Ascending a Fixed Rope (page 139).

The Original Prusik Knot

It is rumoured that this knot was originally invented by a violinist, Dr Karl Prusik, for temporarily repairing violin strings. Quite how true this story is I don't know, suffice to say that it is a useful and well-used knot, and an excellent story!

The basic knot is tied with a loop of thin cord around a thicker rope. The most effective diameter for the loop is 5 mm or 6 mm soft kernmantle. It is quite important to use fairly soft cord as some of the stiffer cords don't grip quite so effectively. It is certainly possible to use thicker cord for the loop but in order to make it work you may have to put in more than the basic two turns around the rope. Remember that each turn you do must go inside the previous one (Photo 16a). It is possible to tie this knot easily with one hand on a taut rope – useful for situations when escaping from the system.

The prusik can cause quite a lot of frustration at times as it tends to tighten up so much in use that it is difficult to release. An effective way to release it after it has been loaded is shown in Photo 16b. Simply roll the loop indicated behind the knot and it will loosen itself. It does not work at all well on wet or icy ropes. On wet ropes it jams severely and on icy ropes it sometimes does not grip at all. Any prusik that tends to slip can be improved by increasing the number of turns around the rope. It must not under any circumstances be used as an autobloc or safety back-up, for once it has been loaded you cannot release it without either cutting it or taking the load off it. It actually works more efficiently on kernmantle ropes if you use hawser laid rope. Number Two nylon is most effective.

In the past people have used the prusik to protect themselves when climbing without a partner. This is done by going around to the top of the cliff and fixing a rope down the intended route. The climber then goes down to the bottom, fixes the other end to an upward-pulling anchor and then attaches on to the rope with a prusik loop. As the climber ascends, the prusik is moved up, thereby affording some security. Whilst it is quite common

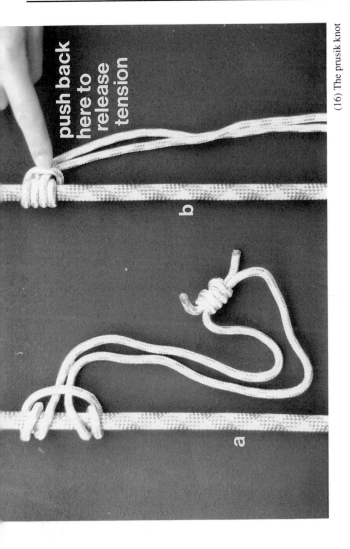

push back
here to
release
tension

b

a

(16) The prusik knot

practice to climb this way you would be advised *never to use a prusik or any other kind of 'prusik' knot for this kind of safety.* Once subjected to a shock loading the loop may well slide down the rope for a short distance and in that movement generate enough heat to melt or fuse it. Either way it is too dangerous to contemplate. A mechanical ascending device is more suited to this task.

It cannot be used effectively when tied in tape.

Useful applications

For ascending a fixed rope

Temporarily securing the rope when escaping from the system (page 144)

The Klemheist

This 'prusik' knot can be tied in cord and has the advantage over the prusik that it can be tied in tape also. In addition, it can be undone more easily after it has been loaded.

Photo 17 shows how to tie the knot. The sling is spiralled around the main rope to create a short loop and a longer loop. It is important that the longer loop is threaded through the shorter loop and the shorter is above the longer. Make sure that all of the turns in the loop lie parallel. Overall it is a much better knot to use than the basic prusik as it causes fewer problems. If using the knot in tape you will find that soft tubular tape works most effectively, though in an emergency the stiffer tapes such as 'Super Blue' work quite well.

You must ensure that the tape lies flat throughout the knot when you tie it. Some distortion always occurs during use but shouldn't cause any problems.

You will find that the Klemheist knot is used quite widely in this book, particularly when we come to discuss glacier travel

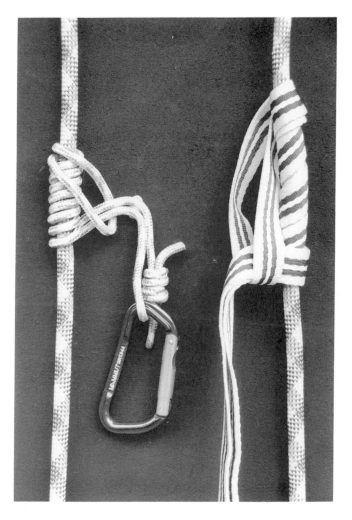

(17) The Klemheist

and crevasse rescue. It is a more efficient alternative to the prusik.

Useful applications

Similar to the prusik knot but can also be tied with a tape sling

The Bachmann

A much used knot but one that I feel has certain limitations. It is effective in use but is prone to distortion and in some cases may prove defective. Its minor disadvantage is that it requires a karabiner – not a problem unless you are short of gear. Photo 18a shows how to tie the knot. The karabiner is often the cause of failure. Its smooth shiny surface comes into contact with the rope so does not actually contribute to the gripping properties of the knot.

It does not work at all on icy ropes!

This is one of a number of knots referred to as *autoblocs*. This means that it is possible to use it in a variety of self-rescue situations as a safety back-up. It will release itself when not under load but lock automatically when a load is applied. Its uses in such situations will be become apparent as you progress through the book.

Useful applications

Same as the prusik (page 44)

As an autobloc

The French Prusik

Of all the 'prusik' knots this is by far and away the most useful. It is sometimes referred to as the 'Johnnyknot' or *the* autobloc. Both terms are incorrect though I'm sure the procurator of the former would be be happy for it to remain as the Johnnyknot. The

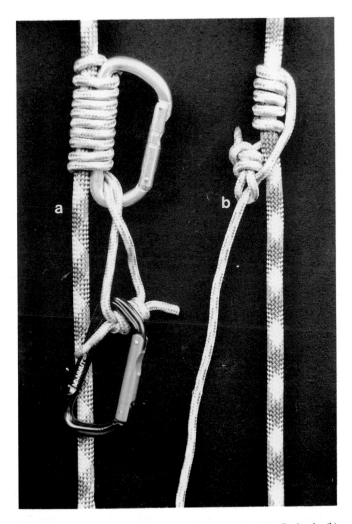

(18) The Bachmann (a) and the Penberthy (b)

latter is incorrect because it is a *an* autobloc. You will find this knot widely used throughout this book. Its prowess in performing many different tasks is unsurpassed by any other knot. Photo 19a shows how the knot is tied.

The best cord to use is 6 mm kernmantle. Make sure that it is good quality and soft as the knot will work even more efficiently. Unlike most of the other prusik knots mentioned this one can easily be released whilst it is under load. For this reason I don't recommend it is used as a knot for ascending the rope. You may inadvertently pull down on it at an inopportune moment and in doing so could cause yourself many problems. To release the knot while it is under load all you need to do is pull the knot firmly but smoothly towards the attachment point (Photo 19b). If for some reason it is difficult to release, a sharp jerk should do the trick. Be careful though as the weight is removed quite suddenly.

Always try to clip the two ends of the loop together with a screwgate krab or two snaplinks back to back (Photo 19). There have been circumstances in which the loops have unclipped themselves from a single snaplink.

Do not be tempted to use it as a lowering device, if the rope starts to run you will not be able to stop it without the knot melting under the heat of the friction generated.

Useful applications

As an autobloc and safety back-up (page 44)

Penberthy knot

This knot is included for the main reason that it does not require a loop sling as all the previous knots do. It can be tied in the same diameter cord as the other knots but has the slight disadvantage that it is time-consuming to tie and cannot be done with one hand. Photo 18b shows how the knot is tied. It also works effectively even when tied with 9 mm rope.

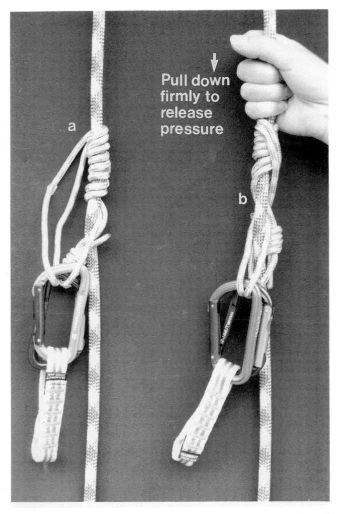

(19) The French prusik

It is one of the few 'prusik' knots that never seems to jam up and that in itself is recommendation enough. However, you will probably find few applications for it in climbing other than in situations where you do not have a 'prusik' loop.

See the final chapter Other Useful Rope 'Tricks' for two applications.

Useful applications

When using the retrievable T-axe belay (page 213)

When using the retrievable ice screw (page 215)

The Alpine Clutch

Though not really a 'prusik' knot of any description, the Alpine clutch is included here because it fits into the family of autoblocs. This is a particularly useful autobloc if you find yourself short of prusik loops. It does however generate a lot of friction and if used in a hoist this often negates some of the mechanical advantage gained in a pulley system.

It works most efficiently on oval shaped karabiners. 'D' shaped krabs not only are less efficient but also jam frequently. If for some reason you do not have oval krabs available try to ensure that you do at least use identical krabs.

To rig the clutch see Photo 20. Clip the rope through both karabiners and decide which is to be the load rope. Take the dead rope, twist it over the load rope karabiner and clip it in. Do not under any circumstances use it as a belaying or abseil device. The rope only moves freely in one direction; it does not move at all in the other.

Useful applications

As an alternative autobloc if no prusiks are available

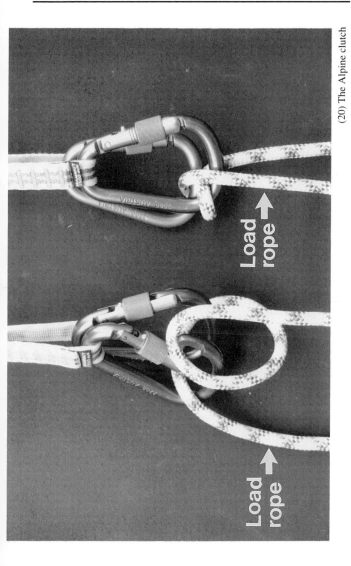

(20) The Alpine clutch

Can also be used for ascending a fixed rope if you only have one prusik loop available (page 143).

BELAYING

This section covers techniques of belaying – the methods of safeguarding a climber's rope whilst he or she is actually climbing. The term 'belaying' is also commonly used to describe the methods of securing oneself to the mountain. To clarify matters in the text the latter is dealt with under the separate heading Tying on to Anchor Points (page 114).

The Belay Plate

This is unquestionably the most commonly used method of safeguarding a climber's rope. It is widely used throughout the world and its popularity is well justified for it is a safe and reliable method of belaying. The days of shoulder belays and waist belays are fading fast. Most certainly the former has almost completely disappeared from the scene. These two methods are discussed later.

The belay plate is available in many different styles. There are those that take single 11 mm rope and those that take combinations of sizes of double ropes. Belay plates with two holes, each capable of taking 9 mm or 11 mm ropes are by far the most versatile. Plates with springs are also available. The spring is intended to reduce the risk of the plate jamming accidentally during use and serves no other purpose except to ensure the plate gets tangled with all your other gear when not in use.

When you buy a belay plate it is necessary to fix a short loop of cord to it. All plates have the facility for this. The length of the piece of cord that you buy should be about 30 cm long and 4 mm or 5 mm diameter. One end is threaded through a small hole in the plate and tied in an overhand knot. Tie an overhand in the other end and use the loop that is formed to clip into the belay karabiner. This cord helps to keep the belay plate in place when

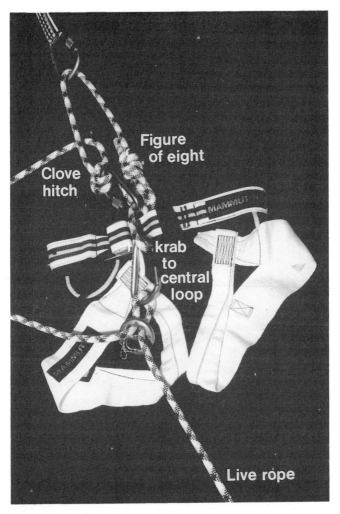

(21) The belay plate

belaying a second and also secures the plate to yourself to help prevent loss.

You will find that a large pear-shaped or oval screwgate karabiner is most useful in conjunction with a belay plate. It is not necessary to use two karabiners, one for each rope, when using double rope for climbing.

When using the plate in the normal manner it should be clipped into the central loop along with all the other anchor tie offs (Photo 21). You should always ensure that there is enough room for you to be able to lock off the plate if your partner falls. Any small or constricted stances may prove quite awkward in manipulating the plate.

If you are on a hanging stance, that is to say one where there is no ledge to stand on and all the belayer's weight must hang off the anchor points, you may find it awkward to belay someone climbing below you. You will find it easier to operate the plate by clipping the live rope through a krab in the anchor so that your second's rope actually travels up through the anchor and down to your belay plate.

The belay plate can also be used on a 'direct belay'. That is attached directly to the anchor. In such cases it is very important that the plate is operated from behind. In this way you will ensure that it can be locked off correctly. It is not possible to do this when standing in front of the plate. (See direct belaying page 174.)

You may find yourself in the situation where you need to tie off the belay plate. This may happen, for example, when escaping from the system (page 144) whilst there is someone hanging on the end of the rope whose weight makes it difficult to release the plate. In this case you should take the controlling rope (ie the one that locks off the plate) back through the karabiner. You will need to make sure that no rope slips through your hands whilst doing this. Once it is threaded through the krab tie at least two half hitches in front of the plate. This will secure the rope and allow you to use both hands for the next stage of the escape.

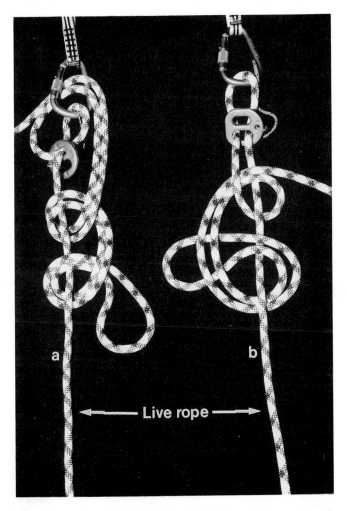

(22) Tying off the belay plate: threading the rope through
the krab (a) and tying off in front of the plate (b)

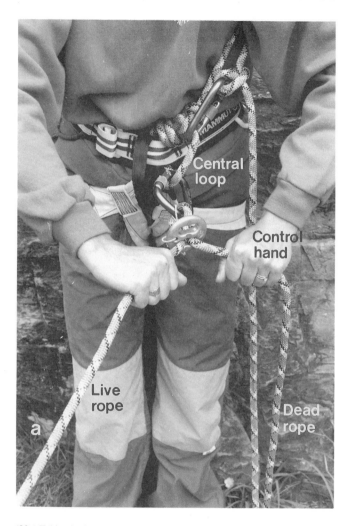

(23a) Taking in the rope using a belay plate – stage one

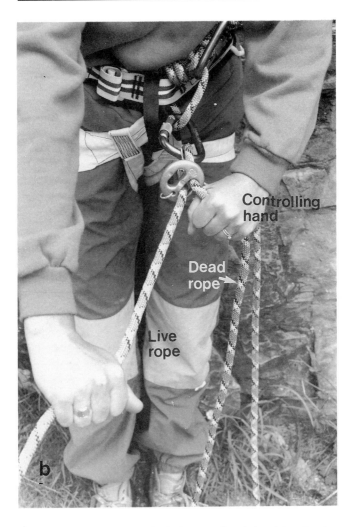

(23b) Taking in the rope using a belay plate – stage two

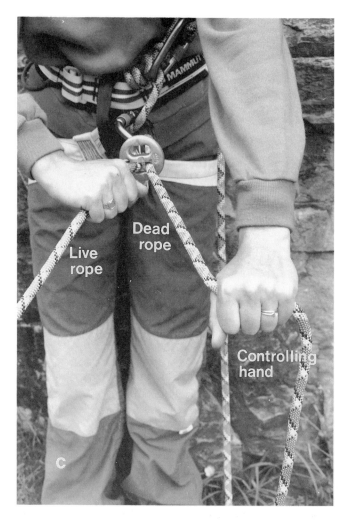

(23c) Taking in the rope using a belay plate – stage three

Tying off the plate in this manner also allows you to untie it whilst it is still under load.

Another way of tying off the plate temporarily is to simply tie a couple of half hitches in front of the plate. This is most useful on a stance where you need to secure your partner whilst gear is sorted out or the guide book consulted. Photo 22 shows both methods clearly.

A third possibility, and one that works better in the latter situation, is to simply tie an overhand knot in the controlling rope. When the knot comes up against the plate it will automatically lock. Do not do this in situations where a load will come on to the plate because unless you are able to take the load off you will not be able to get the knot undone again.

Photos 23a, b and c show the sequence of taking in the rope using a belay plate. This method is applicable to the Lowe belay and figure of eight device mentioned below.

The Lowe belay tube

The Lowe belay tube comes highly recommended and is a very efficient device, both for belaying and abseiling. Unlike the plate it has much less tendency to twist the ropes and can also be used on quite icy ropes where you may not be able to use a plate. Photo 24 shows how to use the tube in the belay system.

It is normal to use the tube with the wider end facing away from the connecting karabiner. If, however, you need to generate a bit more friction, such as in abseiling, you could use it with the wider end towards the connecting karabiner.

The Figure of Eight Descendeur

The figure of eight descendeur can also be used as a belaying device. It is less efficient than plates or tubes but nonetheless performs adequately. There are three ways of using it. The first is to set it up exactly as you would for abseiling. Another is to thread the rope through the small hole and use it in the same way

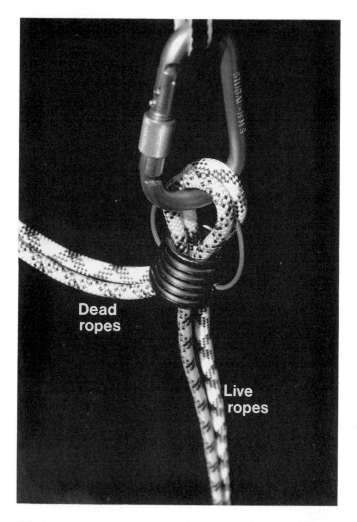

(24) The Lowe belay tube

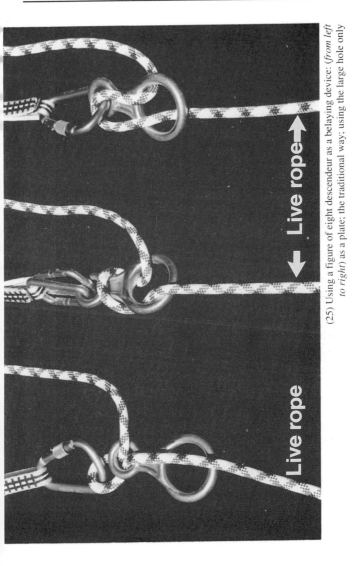

(25) Using a figure of eight descendeur as a belaying device: (*from left to right*) as a plate; the traditional way; using the large hole only

as a plate. The third way is to thread it through the large hole but not through the little hole. Photo 25 shows all three quite clearly.

The problem with the first is that it tends to be awkward to work and twists the ropes. It is also very difficult to operate with double ropes as the individual ropes don't separate easily – paying out or taking in one rope at a time is a problem. If using it as a belay plate it works well but should only really be used with single ropes. The third method of using it works well if it is attached directly to the anchor. It is in common usage on climbs that are well bolted and where the approach is often by abseil so you would carry a figure of eight descendeur in preference to a belay plate. This method works well for bringing up a second but exercise great caution if belaying a leader the same way. You must have upward pulling anchors that are 100% sound.

The figure of eight descendeur is also commonly used when top roping a climber from the ground. It is safer to use it on a direct belay for this purpose rather than attached to the belayer. Be careful if using figure of eight descendeurs as belaying devices when attached directly to the harness. They are particularly awkward to handle.

The Italian Hitch

The Italian hitch can also be used, though again it makes it awkward to handle double ropes and does of course twist the ropes very badly. When using the hitch always try to use a large pear-shaped karabiner as this eases the problems to a significant extent. See page 20 for relevant notes on the Italian hitch.

Body Belays

There are two types of body belay: the shoulder belay and the waist belay. The former is almost extinct but is still occasionally used. The latter, though less commonly seen these days, is fairly widely used but by comparison to mechanical methods of belaying they are considered old fashioned.

The Waist Belay

If you were to show a beginner a body belay and a mechanical belaying device, such as the belay plate, not only would it take them a much shorter time to master the plate, it would also be very much safer to use. Bearing this in mind I consider the waist belay to be a fairly advanced belaying technique and one that in unpractised hands is dangerous.

There are some important considerations to take into account. Firstly, to have any hope of holding a severe fall, gloves must be worn. Long sleeves and good padding around the back are also necessary. This means that on hot, sunny, windless days you can't just wear a T-shirt – unless of course you are happy to run the risk of sustaining terrible rope burns.

Years ago when I worked at Idwal Cottage Youth Hostel, two girls came in early one afternoon and asked if we could be of help. One of the girls had her hands tucked under her armpits, the other could barely walk. As the tale unfolded we discovered that they had decided to 'have a go' at rock climbing and acquired a rope, but no other gear. They spotted some people climbing on the Gribin Facet, though of course they didn't know its name, and thought they'd go up there. The first girl, the one with her hands in her armpits, had climbed up, sat on the top and told her friend to follow. Unfortunately near the top her friend fell and she was unable to stop the rope from sliding through her hands. Her friend tumbled all the way to the bottom of the cliff, but not too fast because she held on to the rope all the way. It is sufficient to say that the rope burns were pretty horrible.

Secondly, you should always bring the rope over your head when putting it around your waist. 'Stepping' into it often leads to tangles and if you fail to hold a falling second the rope can be pulled down around your knees. By looping it over your head the ropes to the anchor prevent it sliding down below your waist.

When operating the waist belay you will have a 'live' rope and a 'dead' or 'controlling' rope. The live rope has the other climber directly on the end of it and the dead rope goes to the pile of slack rope you have beside you.

Always twist the dead rope around the arm that holds it and under no circumstances let go of it. *Never* twist the live rope around your arm – any sudden load may snap your arm.

If you are tied to an anchor point via the front of your harness, make sure that the live rope comes around on the same side as the rope from the anchor. Photos 26a, b and c show the technique for taking in the rope safely. Any loading will then twist you into the anchor rather than out of it which may cause you to let go of the rope.

When belaying the leader always arrange your stance so that if the person falls they do not fall in such a way that the rope comes away from your waist. This means that if you are facing into the crag you must make sure that the live rope comes out on the opposite side of your body that the load is likely to come from. If you are facing out from the crag, the live rope must come around on the same side that you anticipate the load to come from and twist your body slightly towards that side. For extra safety the live rope could be clipped into a karabiner on a strong point of the harness somewhere near the central loop. Always make sure that you have sufficient space to be able to lock off the rope in the correct manner for holding a fall.

If you have to escape from the system (page 144) when using the waist belay, you can release both hands if you wrap the controlling rope repeatedly around your leg and finally stand on it to trap it. This is terribly uncomfortable so make sure that you work quickly!

The Shoulder Belay

This method of body belaying, illustrated in Photo 27 is most useful for hauling people up climbs and for quick belays when moving together. It is important that it is set up as illustrated, with the live rope coming from underneath the armpit. If it comes over

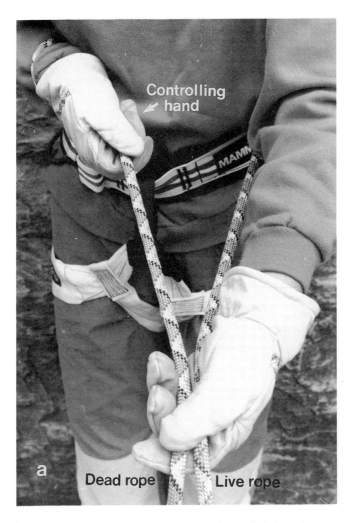

(26a) Taking in the rope using a waist belay – stage one

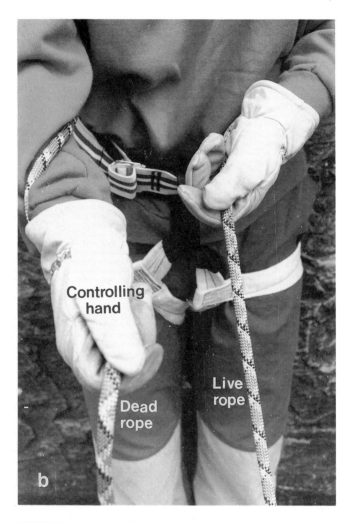

(26b) Taking in the rope using a waist belay – stage two

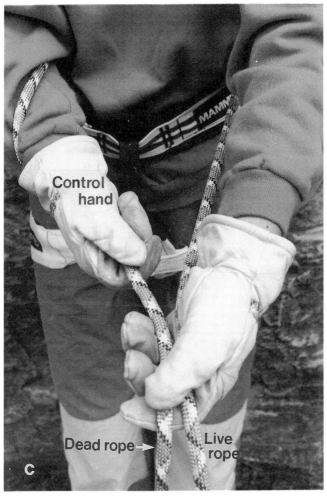

(26c) Taking in the rope using a waist belay – stage three
Then return to (a) and repeat the sequence

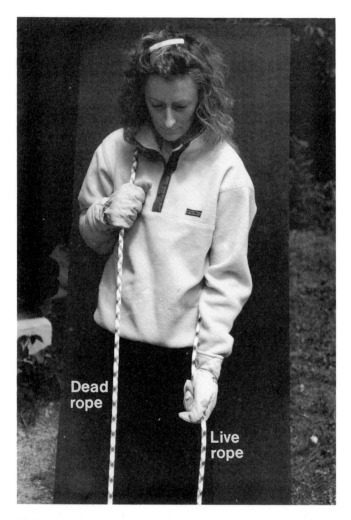

(27) The shoulder belay

your shoulder any loading on it will tip you forward and may pull
the rope off. You need to be well braced, preferably leaning
against the rock, with the leg on the same side as the live rope
braced slightly forward. You *must not* use this method for
belaying a leader.

LOWERING

Most of the times you go down on a rope will either be by
climbing down or by abseil. There could, however, be the odd
occasion where you need to be lowered down by your partner.
Such an occasion could be as part of a rescue or perhaps when
you are descending but are a little unsure of what lies ahead. If
you are being lowered you can go down to see what's ahead and,
should you discover that the route is impassable your partner can
belay you while you climb back up without having to change the
belay system at all.

   The device that you use for lowering could be a figure of
eight, a belay plate, karabiner brake, Italian hitch or any other
suitable method. For notes on these please refer to the appropriate part of the book.

   Whichever device or knot you choose to use, it is worth
putting on a French prusik safety back-up. This is attached to the
live rope and thence to the anchor. Putting this on allows you to
rest and take both hands off the controlling rope if you need to,
though if you intend leaving the lower for some time you should
tie the device off by an appropriate method (Photo 28).

   To convert a lower into a belay to bring a climber back up
as in the situation quoted, all you need to do is pull the rope
through the lowering device instead of letting it out. You don't
even need to take the French prusik safety back-up off.

Passing a Knot

If, on a rescue for example, you need to join two ropes together
you can pass the knot through a lowering device fairly simply.

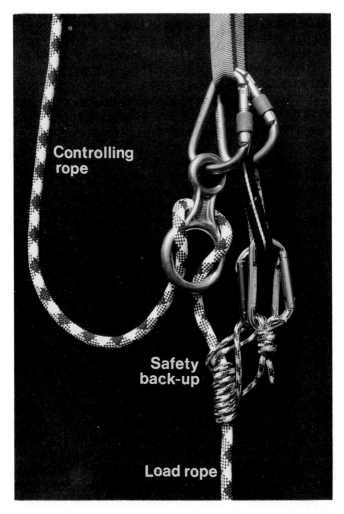

(28) The French prusik being used as a safety back–up on a lower

The technique for this is essentially the same as that described for abseiling past a knot (page 135 and Photo 61). With the safety back-up already on, allow the joining knot to come about 30 cm from the lowering device. This must coincide with all the load coming on to the safety back up. Take the rope out of the device and put the rope back in with the knot below and having theoretically passed through the device. Make sure that the knot is hard up against the device and gradually lower the load back on by gently releasing the autobloc a little at a time. Once the load is back on, release the autobloc to allow the knot to pass by and then put it back on again. Make sure that the autobloc is long enough to allow the load to come back on to the device after passing the knot.

Another method of passing the knot is illustrated in Photos 29a and b. The system is identical to that previously described except that a Mariner's knot and prusik is used in place of the French prusik. Allow the joining knot to come 30 cm from the lowering device, put on the prusik and then tie the Mariner's knot, take the load on the prusik, pass the knot and gradually release the Mariner by allowing it to untwist itself slowly. Please note that for the Mariner's knot to work efficiently you must have quite a long prusik loop.

Cowstail

A cowstail is a short attachment from the harness that can be used to clip into an anchor point without having to use the rope to tie in. It must be attached to a part of the harness that will safely support your weight without relying on the rope.

It is possible to buy pre-stitched slings that have a number of different loops to which you can attach yourself. These are sometimes called 'snake' slings. An item of equipment such as this is indispensable in self-rescue situations. If however, you are not so fortunate to own a snake sling, one can easily be improvised from a tape sling or quick draws.

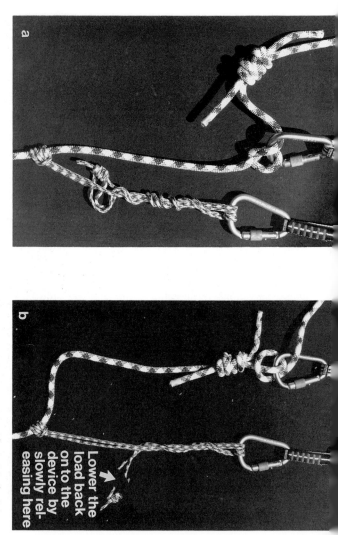

(29) Passing a knot through a lowering device using the Mariner's knot

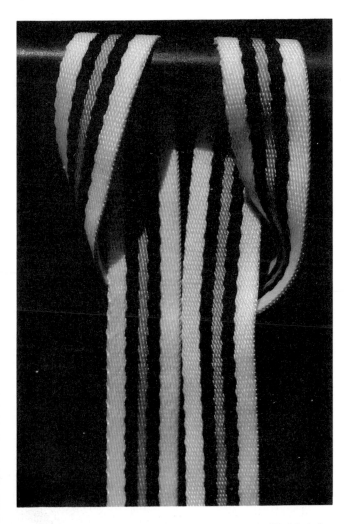

(30) A larksfoot

Larksfoot

This is the term used to describe a method of securing a sling to an anchor (Photo 30). It is quick and convenient to do but in some instances, such as extending wire runners, it is very dangerous to use. I include it here because I mention its use in other situations later in this book. It is most useful when ascending a fixed rope or 'prusiking' (page 139) to secure the foot loop.

THE HANGING HOIST

This technique, as with many others in the book, is described as an individual exercise that forms a part of a larger operation. If you have a victim who is hanging on the end of a rope and you wish to release the rope from their harness, you have a number of options.

The first option to consider is to get the victim to stand on a ledge or foothold nearby and take enough weight off the rope to allow you to untie it. *Remember* though that you should attach the victim into the new rope or anchor point before untying the original rope.

If the victim is unable to help you in any way or is hanging free, the second option, having already clipped the victim into the new tie-on or anchor, is to simply cut the rope near the original tie-on. Be very careful if you choose this option, for two reasons. Firstly, there will be a lot of ropes and general mêlée around you and the victim so be sure that you cut the right rope. Secondly, when a rope is under tension a sharp knife will cut it cleanly and surprisingly easily, so be careful not to slip with the knife and cut other ropes as well.

The third option available to you is more complicated than the previous two, but is the one you are most likely to have to use. Photo 31 shows the basic set-up for this technique. Proceed as follows: abseil down until your feet are level with the victim's chest and lock off so you don't go any further. Put a prusik loop (a short one) on the victim's rope and clip in a krab. Pass a long

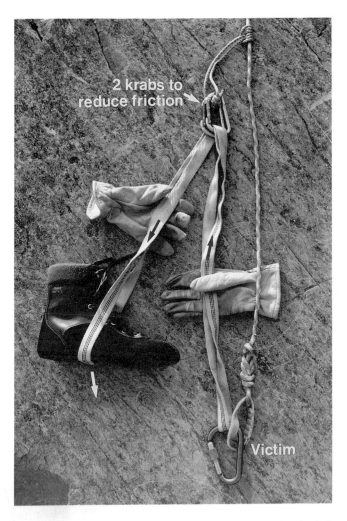

(31) The hanging hoist

sling through the krab and clip one end of it to the victim's harness – *not* into the central loop. If you put your foot into the other end of the sling and pull the victim up with your arms, at the same time pushing down hard with your leg, the victim will move up surprisingly easily and their weight will come off the end of the rope. You must find some way to keep the victim's weight off the old end of rope whilst you untie it. This could be done by putting a French prusik on the victim's new rope (which will already be tied in) and attaching it to another prusik on your own rope or fixing it to your person. This temporarily holds the victim whilst you untie the old rope and you can then lower him or her on to the new rope by releasing the French prusik. Alternatively, if you have an assistant at the top of the new rope they can take in the rope tightly as you effect the hanging hoist and when you release the load from the foot sling the victim drops on to the new rope.

Remember that whichever option you choose you must always attach the victim to the new rope or anchor before untying the original rope.

COILING THE ROPE

The 'traditional' way of coiling a rope is illustrated in Photos 32. Unfortunately most modern ropes do not comply very well with this method. Unless you deliberately try to take the twists out of the rope it will not lie flat and neatly coiled as illustrated. However, forcing the twists out of the rope can do harm to the long-term durability and handling properties of the rope. It is much better to allow the rope to twist as it wants to than to make it do something that's not good for it. A better method is illustrated in Photos 33. This is known as 'lap coiling' and it is much better for the rope. The sequence shows how to coil a rope this way and how to finish the coiling off. The spare rope left after coiling can be used to tie the rope to your back, leaving your hands free to hold on to the rock.

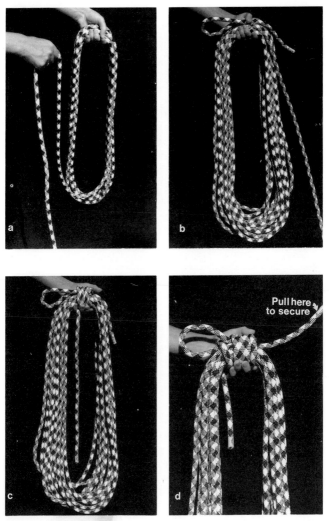

(32) Coiling a rope in the traditional way

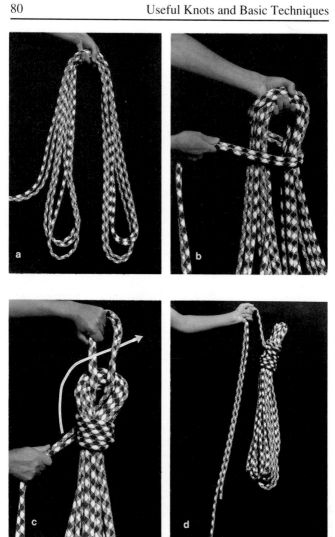

(33) Lap coiling

IMPROVISED HARNESSES

The vast majority of modern-day climbers use a purpose-made harness of one kind or another: a sit harness, simple waist belt or full body harness. Nevertheless, you may find yourself in a situation one day that requires an improvised harness. A typical example is if you are climbing with a party that only have waist belts and you decide to do a bit of abseiling with them. Another occasion might be in glacier travel when you only have a sit harness and feel a chest harness combined with a sit harness would be safer.

It is well worth bringing to your attention here that it is not possible for anyone to hang on the end of a rope by the waist for more than a few minutes without causing great discomfort, asphyxiation after about ten minutes and death within twenty minutes. You should, therefore, never lower or abseil off a direct waist tie.

A simple method of relieving the weight off a waist tie is to clip a long sling on to the main climbing rope with a karabiner, slide it down until it is up against the waist tie and stand in it. This is of course only a temporary solution to the problem and a more comfortable harness should be rigged as soon as possible.

Sit Slings

The Dulfer seat is probably the most commonly used improvised sit sling. It requires a 2.4 m sling for the average-sized person.

Pass the sling behind the back but do not step into it at all. The knot or sewn join should be positioned in the middle of the back. Pull a loop either side of your body and one up between your legs. Clip all three loops together at the front with a large screwgate karabiner (Photo 34a). For extra security the three loops could be clipped into the waist tie or belt. On small people the tape can be tucked up through the waist belt and turned around a few times to take up the slack. There is no safety or

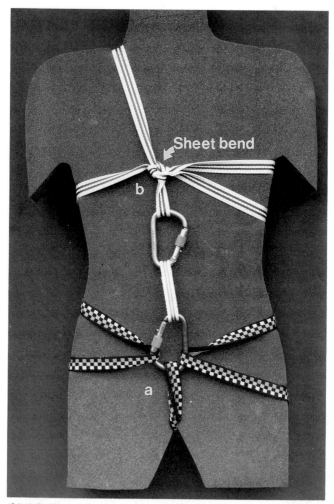

(34) A Dulfer seat (a) and Parisienne baudrier (b) connected
to make an improvised full body harness

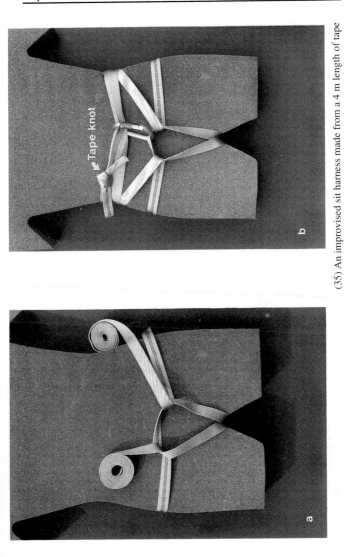

(35) An improvised sit harness made from a 4 m length of tape

comfort in a Dulfer sling that is continually falling around the knees.

If for some reason your sling is not long enough to go around the person, a simple and effective sit sling can be arranged by twisting the sling once to form a figure of eight. Step one leg into each loop and bring the centre up to clip into the waist belt or tie. Any slack can be taken up and tied in a knot on one side.

The Dulfer seat is really only of use provided that it is under constant tension. It's not worth using it as an alternative to a proper sit harness for general mountaineering. It slips down around the legs and is generally very awkward. An interesting and more comfortable, longer lasting sit harness can be constructed with a 4-4.5 m length of tape. The wider the tape the more comfortable the harness. Photos 35a and b show how to rig this up. The ends are joined together using the tape knot. Whilst it is longer lasting than the Dulfer it is not comfortable to hang in for a long time as the leg loops squeeze and cut into the thighs.

A third improvisation is illustrated in Photo 36. This requires two short slings (120 cm). Tie an overhand knot about two-thirds of the way along each sling and step one leg into each of the larger loops. Thread the waist belt through the two shorter loops of the slings or clip them to a krab on the belt and make sure that when you tie on you thread the rope through both slings and the waist belt. If you do not have a waist belt you could use a third sling around the waist instead or even the end of the rope.

Chest Harnesses

In Britain climbers rarely have cause to resort to wearing a chest harness. Perhaps the only time that you would certainly use one is in an emergency situation involving the lowering of a victim (see Assisted Evacuation page 164). In such cases a chest harness makes it more comfortable for the victim and indeed may also make it more comfortable for the rescuer.

In Alpine regions, however, where a fall into a crevasse may result in a climber hanging free, some kind of chest support is

(36) A sit harness made from two short slings
connected to the waist belt for security

essential. The reasons for this are quite simple – the centre of gravity of the human frame is at the sternum and wearing a rucksack makes the body top-heavy. The more weight in a rucksack the more top-heavy the climber is. The attachment point of a sit harness is very much lower than the centre of gravity so that in a fall into space, particularly, the climber is likely to tip upside down and may even fall out of the harness. There are ways of gaining chest support by the manner in which the rope is tied to the climber (see Moving Together page 184). However satisfactory these methods may seem, they are never as convenient as a properly rigged chest harness, improvised or otherwise.

Parisienne Baudrier

The simplest but most effective chest harness to improvise is the Parisienne baudrier. It requires a 2.4 m sling of at least 2.5 cm wide tape. If you are able to get 5 cm tape the overall harness will be more comfortable to wear.

To tie the harness, pass one arm through the sling and bring the rest of the sling under the opposite armpit. Tie a sheet bend in the manner illustrated in Photo 4. It is very important to ensure that you *do not* pass the end of the sling through the loop that goes over the shoulder. If you do the resulting knot will be a slip knot and any load will only tighten the sling around the body causing eventual asphyxiation and possibly death. The harness should be snug but not tight enough to cause restricted movement. After tying the knot there should be at least a large enough loop to clip a karabiner in (Photo 34b).

To be absolutely truthful, there are few other improvised chest harnesses that are as effective. Crossed sling baudriers and others that may have been suggested in the past make poor and dangerous alternatives.

The most likely problem that you will encounter with the Parisienne baudrier is that the sling may not be long enough to go around the chest. It is a simple matter to rectify this by adding

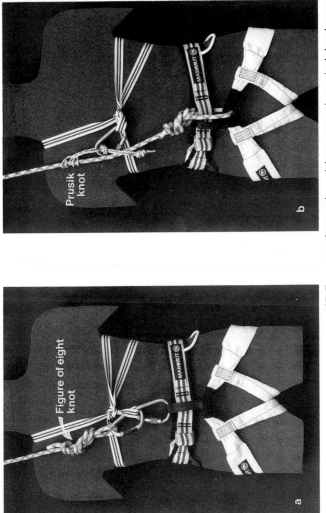

(37) Two ways of connecting a sit harness to an improvised chest harness

another shorter sling on to the part of the sling that comes under the armpit. This will allow extra tape for tying the sheet bend.

Improvised Body Harness

The Dulfer seat or any of the other improvised sit harnesses and Parisienne baudrier can be connected together to make a full body harness. There are a number of ways of doing this, the choice of method depending on the situation you find yourself in and the equipment available to you. If you have a long enough loop after tying the sheet bend on the Parisienne baudrier, clip the loop into the Dulfer seat karabiner thus connecting the two together. Photos 37a and b show ways to connect a purpose-made sit harness to an improvised chest harness and two different methods of attaching the rope. Similar methods can be employed for an improvised sit harness.

DOUBLE ROPE TECHNIQUE

The use of two ropes in most climbing scenarios allows greater flexibility in the protection of both leader and second, and also in dealing with emergencies or retreating from the mountain. Whilst tangles inevitably occur (no matter how experienced the climbers), by adopting a fairly logical and thoughtful approach such annoyances can be kept to a minimum.

The choice of diameter of rope must be left to the individual. Sometimes two 8.8 mm ropes, or even thinner, may be sufficient. At other times combinations of thick and thin may fit the bill. Rarely, however, will two 11 mm ropes be necessary. Remember that there are certain standards and recommendations made by the international safety body, the UIAA, concerning the different uses to which a rope may be put.

When using double ropes for climbing, try to make sure that you begin the day with the ropes free of any tangles, twists or kinks. When placing running belays on a climb, try to keep one rope for runners to your left and the other for runners to your right. Often this will mean looking carefully at the route prior to setting off and doing a bit of careful planning. On stances, try to run both ropes through to check for tangles before setting off again. Run them through individually if possible.

When using a belay plate to safeguard another climber, both ropes can be clipped into the same karabiner. Attaching to multiple anchor points is very much simpler – use one rope for each anchor.

Snow, Rock and Ice Anchors

In this chapter I propose to discuss mainly the methods that can be employed to tie on to various types of anchor. It is not really within the remit of this book to discuss at length the methods of placement of anchors; however I think that there are one or two aspects that merit discussion.

ANCHORS ON ROCK

Anchors on or in rock can be fashioned many different ways. From simple slings to bolts; from Friends to nuts; from pitons to trees. Anything that is secure enough to hold the party to the mountain will suffice, provided that it is ethically acceptable of course.

However, when you create an anchor on rock, or snow and ice for that matter, consider firstly what you require of that anchor. It goes without saying that it must be able to hold everyone to the mountain, but consider also the direction that the load may be coming from. A sling draped over a small spike at your feet will not hold an upward pulling force such as that experienced when holding a leader fall. Consider also how much force you expect to come on to an anchor. It's no good expecting an RP size 0 to hold the weight of two climbers during an assisted evacuation. So often accidents occur as a result of the party having paid little attention to their own safety when rigging up anchors. Tragically, some end in death.

Nuts or Chocks

These come in an enormous variety of shapes and sizes these days – too many to mention individually.

When placing any nut in a crack, do so with careful thought. It's all very well to say that here of course – when you're hanging on by fingertips halfway up an overhanging wall somewhere, it's a whole different ball game. Make sure that there is plenty of

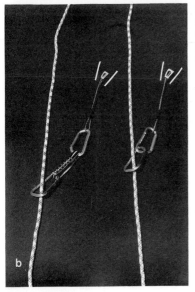

(38) Nuts placed in opposition to each other (a). Such a set-up is not safe unless both nuts are well placed. The correct way to extend wire runners (b)

rock around the nut so that any load will tighten it in to the crack. Make sure too that extracting it will be a simple matter. When used as running belays you will also have to make sure that they are well seated so that the rope running through a karabiner does not lift the nut out.

Any small nuts should ideally be threaded with wire. Any nuts that take cord thinner than 7 mm will be considerably less strong than the same nut threaded with wire. Wire nuts will often need to be extended to reduce leverage and the possibility that they might come out at an inopportune moment. Always extend wire runners by connecting the extension to the wire with a karabiner. Connecting with a sling directly around the wire is unacceptably dangerous (Photo 38b). You may of course have to extend any running belay from time to time and the same theory applies.

Nuts in opposition to each other can sometimes provide a satisfactory anchor or runner where otherwise you would have nothing. When rigging such an anchor you must be absolutely certain that the forces involved in loading will not pull the nuts out of the crack (Photo 38a). If one nut fails, the other is almost certain to fail too.

Nut placement is something of a science, study it carefully and learn well.

Slings

To use a sling is one of the oldest methods of anchoring used in climbing. It is well worth considering buying pre-stitched slings. They are much more convenient than the knotted variety. Unlike a knot the stitching cannot work loose or slip through itself. However there may be the odd occasion where a knotted sling would be of use and it is certainly worth carrying a couple when mountaineering.

Slings come in a variety of sizes from quick draws through to 2.4 m slings and from lightweight tubular tape to heavier 'super' tape. Slings can also of course be made out of rope,

(39a) A sling stretched too tightly over a block

(39b) A much safer anchor

though they are seen much less commonly these days. There are a few special considerations to take into account. The most important one worth mentioning is that if using a sling draped over a spike or flake or threaded around a rock or tree, you must make sure that it is not stretched too tightly around the object. A sling placed such is considerably weaker than one that has some slack in it (Photos 39a and b). Make sure that there are no sharp edges to cut into the material.

Friends

The invention of Friends and, more recently, other devices along the same lines has revolutionized protection for climbers. A well-placed Friend is as strong and reliable as a well placed nut or sling around a spike. Like all gear they take a bit of practice to get used to. Take care not to cram the cams into a crack as they can be difficult, if not impossible, to remove.

Pitons

Pitons are not commonly used in the UK these days. The old expression 'that a man who would use a piton on British rock would shoot foxes' has kept their use to a minimum. However, they are in popular usage in winter climbing and in Alpine mountaineering.

One would most commonly encounter a piton in an 'in situ' position on the mountain. If that be the case you must establish that it looks strong enough to be used safely. Sometimes pitons have been in situ for a good many years and though they may appear outwardly strong, underneath all sorts of corrosion may have taken place. Some years ago I was climbing the East Wall Girdle on the side of the Idwal Slabs. On that route there was a semi-hanging belay, the main anchor being an in situ piton. There was already a climber on the stance and so there was no room for me. After a short wait he began to vacate the stance and I moved into position. I thought that it would be prudent to check out the piton anchor so put in a sling and krab and pulled on it pretty violently. The head snapped off completely. The previous incumbents of the stance had been tied solely to that piton.

When placing pitons choose a crack into which at least the first quarter of the piton can be placed by hand. Having done that, hammer it in until it makes a high ringing sound. Any placement that makes a dull thudding sound is usually less secure and a fatter but shorter peg may be needed. If the piton reaches a point where it refuses to go any further, do not persist in hammering it to death but tie it off in a similar manner to that illustrated in Photo 49b page 112. Make sure that you tie it off as close to the rock as possible to reduce the leverage.

ANCHORS ON SNOW

Generally speaking always try to use rock anchors as they are much more reliable. There will, however, be occasions when it simply will not be possible to select a rock anchor. In such cases a variety of snow anchors are available. On a cautionary note you should remember that snow is not as predictable in quality as rock. A seemingly sound anchor may well fail when put to the test. Having said that, if you are able to arrange an anchor in good compact snow and it is set up correctly, there is no reason why it shouldn't hold a substantial load.

Ice Axe Anchor

In its simplest form an ice axe anchor can be arranged by driving the axe vertically into the snow. It is necessary to have a consistently sound snow pack for this to work efficiently. There should not be any weak underlying layers in the snow which may cause failure under load. Occasionally it may not be possible to get the ice axe the whole length of the shaft, in which case it should be tied off at the snow to reduce leverage.

If the snow is not so compact it may be better to use a buried ice axe anchor. The horizontally buried axe illustrated in Photo

(40) A horizontally buried ice
axe in a T-slot *left*.
Detail of the horizontally
buried axe *below*.
The sling is clove hitched
around the shaft

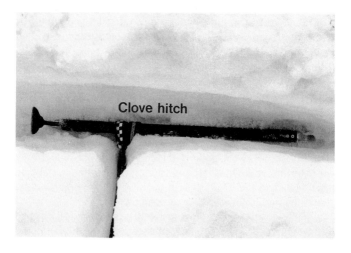

Clove hitch

40 makes a fairly effective anchor in reasonably compact snow. It is necessary to cut down fairly deeply into the snow pack and to cut a small trench to accommodate the sling attachment point. When you are cutting out the slot for the axe take great care not to disturb the snow in front of the anchor. This is integral to the reliability of the anchor.

When you attach a sling to the shaft of the ice axe, do so before you put the axe in and attach it about two-thirds of the way along from the spike to the head and make sure you place the pick down into the snow.

Photo 41a shows a much stronger method of making an anchor but it is of course one that requires two axes. This method is called the T-axe for obvious reasons. Having cut out the slot for your horizontal axe (still bearing in mind the above considerations), you simply take the second ice axe and drive it in slightly back from the vertical, behind the horizontal axe. The sling should go on first of course and should be clove hitched around the shaft. Ideally the vertical axe should be driven right to the head but if this is not possible it can be tied off at the level of the horizontal axe. The sling should come over the top of the horizontal axe so that any loading helps to hold it in place.

Various combinations, such as the horizontal behind the vertical, are possible (Photo 41b). Note that in all cases the vertical axe is placed close to the head of the horizontal axe rather than centrally.

If you are using two tools and one is shorter than the other it is generally better to place the shorter one as the horizontal axe.

Once the anchor is set up and in position it is sometimes necessary to fill in the slot with snow and stamp it down firmly to make sure that the gear remains buried.

A large stance should be cut downhill of the anchor and you must sit down to belay. You may have to get well below the anchor for it to work effectively.

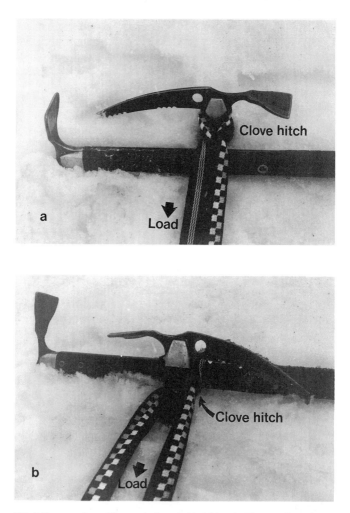

(41) A T-axe anchor with a vertical axe behind (a) and a T-axe anchor with vertical axe in front (b). In both cases the sling is attached to the rear axe

Other Buried Items!

It is possible to secure yourself to almost anything buried in a slot or trench in the snow. Though highly unlikely I have heard people say that it is possible to anchor to a buried glove! A rucksack is certainly a feasible option. Make sure that you take out any gear that you need before you bury it though. A sling can be clove hitched around the body of the sack and to create extra length additional slings can be added. The sling is then run out of the T-slot and you attach yourself to this point. As with buried axes be careful not to disturb the snow in front of the slot. You should also stomp some snow over the top and bury the rucksack completely.

The Deadman Anchor

The Deadman is a spade-shaped plate made of alloy and has a wire fixing to which all anchor attachments are made. A smaller version, the Deadboy, is available. It is a popular type of snow anchor among British climbers but not so throughout the rest of the world. Placed correctly they provide solid, reliable anchors. Unfortunately, placement is so critical that they often fail under the lightest of loadings. In addition they are the most awkward item of climbing equipment to carry that has ever been invented.

To place the Deadman as an anchor you should proceed as follows. Cut a slot across the slope; this should be quite deep, depending on the quality of snow. The poorer the snow, the deeper the slot. You must now cut a second slot down the hill at 90 degrees to the first. This is to accommodate the wire strop.

Take an imaginary line at 90 degrees to the angle of the slope and bisect it with the Deadman. Tilt the Deadman a little closer to the upper slope and then hammer it into the snow until it is at least 30 cm below the bottom of the trench. It is important that you maintain the angle of 40 degrees as you hammer it in . Any other angle may cause the anchor to fail under load.

Once in position you must tie yourself into the strop. Any of the methods described in Tying on to Anchors (page 114) is suitable. You must, however, remember to stay well below the slot that the Deadman was placed in originally. This may mean that you have to go down the hill for 3 or even 5 m. The reason for this is that the angle between the wire and the plate should not exceed 50 degrees. You should cut out a deep hole and sit in it to belay. Make sure that you also have something to brace your feet against.

It is hardly surprising when you consider all the critical factors of placement, that the Deadman plate is not popular.

Snow Stake

A method of fashioning an anchor in snow that is used widely in New Zealand. It is becoming more common worldwide now. Basically this is a piece of 'angle iron' but made of alloy and with a point at one end and holes for attachment at the other. The stake is driven slightly back from the vertical with the point of the 'V' shape facing the direction of pull. It can also be placed horizontally in a T-slot.

The Snow Bollard

Surprisingly enough, the snow bollard can be a very effective anchor. They are most commonly used as abseil anchors in situations where there is nothing else available and you wish to leave no equipment behind. They can be used equally well of course, as anchors from which to belay (Photo 42).

The snow bollard is prepared by cutting a teardrop shape in the snow with the point of the teardrop pointing towards where the load is expected to come from. The trench that is cut around the shape should be cut much deeper at the top than at the bottom. It should also be undercut slightly to enable the rope to sit more securely. The widest diameter of the bollard is determined by the quality of the snow that it is cut into. Basically the poorer the quality of snow, the wider the bollard.

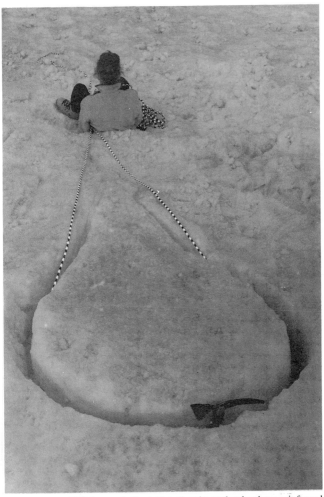

(42) A snow bollard. Note that the anchor has been reinforced with an ice axe and that the belayer sits well below the anchor

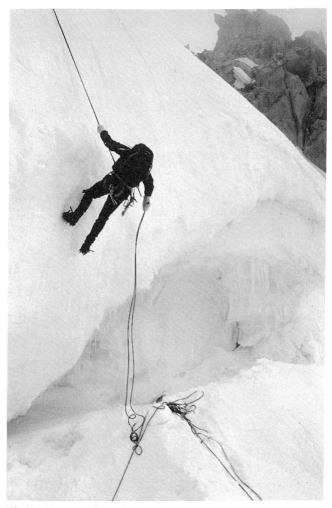

(43) Abseiling over a bergschrund. A bollard was used as an anchor

The rope, when placed around the bollard, tends to work a bit like a cheese wire and if the snow is not especially solid it will quite simply pull through. To alleviate the problem slightly, the back of the bollard can be padded with a rucksack, ice axe or, if you are using it to retreat from, anything that you are prepared to leave behind. If you do have to use a very large snow bollard to retreat from, you will probably find that the amount of friction generated by the rope is enough to prevent you from being able to recover the ropes after abseiling. To alleviate the problem to a certain extent, quickly see-saw the rope back and forth around the bollard just before you set off. This creates an icy groove which the rope will slide into more easily.

You will almost always have to use the rope directly around the anchor to secure yourself, so use any of the methods appropriate in the section Tying on to Anchors (page 114). As with the Deadman you must cut your stance well below the anchor and sit down to belay.

Foot Belays

These techniques are particularly effective for safeguarding someone climbing up from below or someone descending. They can also be usefully employed in glacier travel for safeguarding someone who is making an exploratory manoeuvre among crevasses.

The New Zealand boot axe belay is effective in good hard snow. Photo 44 shows the technique being used. Note that the pick of the axe points forward and one hand remains pushing it into the snow. Friction, which enables you to take the strain, is generated by increasing the amount of rope in contact with the ankle. Do not be tempted to wrap the rope around the ankle to increase the friction. Some weight should remain on the leg that braces against the axe.

A variation of this technique is to use the rope in the manner illustrated in Photo 45a. Here the loaded rope is passed underneath the boot and then around the ankle to create friction. To

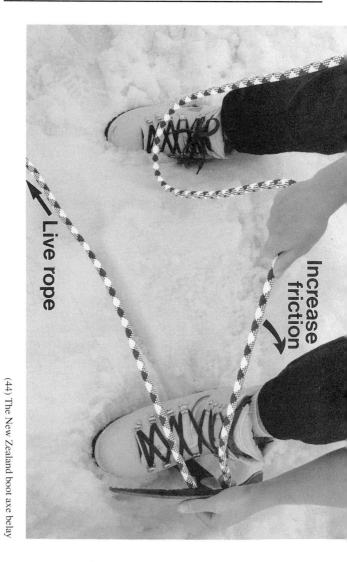

Live rope

Increase friction

(44) The New Zealand boot axe belay

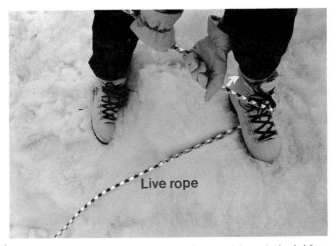

Live rope

(45a) The boot belay. Keep all your weight on the loaded foot.
Increase the friction by wrapping the rope around the ankle.

(45b) The boot belay. An ice axe is added for extra security

begin with you have to make a small platform for your foot and cut a small slot for the rope to pass through. The platform can be stomped out but the slot needs to be cut. In soft snow stomp down until you have a firm platform. Make sure that you keep some weight on the leg that has the rope wrapped around it as this will help to hold your foot in place whilst you are safeguarding someone. It is usually sufficient to use just the foot but an ice axe can be inserted if you need extra security (Photo 45b). On the whole this is a safer and more effective variation of the New Zealand foot brake.

A third method, popularly called the 'stomper belay', is effective in a surprising number of instances but will be found most useful for safeguarding a partner on easy-angled terrain; when probing for crevasses for example. The ice axe is driven vertically into the snow and a karabiner is clipped through the hole in the head. The rope to your partner passes through this krab and is safeguarded using a shoulder belay whilst standing on the head of the axe. Make sure that you stand well braced to take a load as it would be catastrophic if the rope were to slip off your shoulder (Photo 46). If you want to use this method on steeper slopes, the shoulder belay makes it quite unstable. Instead, you could belay the rope off your harness using a belay plate or Italian hitch.

It is a popular myth that some of the techniques described here can be employed to save a falling partner in an emergency when moving together. The New Zealand foot brake we are told, for instance, is used most effectively to stop someone by throwing all the coils away and driving the axe into the snow with the rope wrapped around it (as illustrated in Photo 44) and to gradually slow the falling climber by increasing the friction on the belay. Not only is this dangerous, it is also impossible to achieve except in situations where it is deliberately set up as a demonstration. Apart from anything else, by discarding the coils you are giving your falling partner more rope with which to gather momentum which immediately decreases the chances of

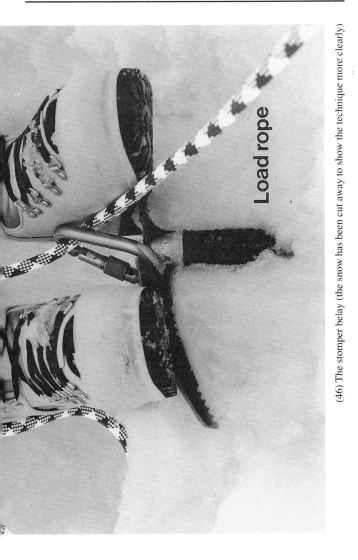

Load rope

(46) The stomper belay (the snow has been cut away to show the technique more clearly)

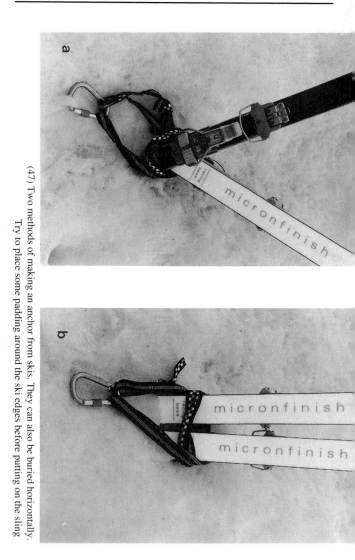

(47) Two methods of making an anchor from skis. They can also be buried horizontally. Try to place some padding around the ski edges before putting on the sling

holding the fall. The safest way and the best chance of holding a falling climber is to move on a short rope with few coils and be ready to correct a slip before it becomes a fall. On ridges the old saying 'if you fall into France I'll jump into Italy' is the most effective way to stop a fall. It does require quick reactions and plenty of 'bottle' however. See Moving Together page 184.

Skis

Though it may seem somewhat out of place to discuss ski anchors here, many of the the rope techniques described in this book are applicable to ski touring.

There are three main types of ski anchors. Photos 47a and b shows two of the types. Note that in both methods the skis are tilted back slightly from the vertical. This makes them mechanically more sound and able to take a load more efficiently. In the example where the skis are parallel, the soles face outwards towards the load and in the crossed ski anchor the soles face each other. In both cases you should make an attempt to put some kind of padding over the sharp edges of the skis. In snow of a poor, unconsolidated nature or very soft snow, the skis can be buried horizontally in much the same way as other buried items. The attachment sling goes around the centre of the bindings and the skis are buried together sole to sole.

ICE ANCHORS

The most reliable type of anchor to use in good ice is the ice screw. They come in a variety of shapes and sizes. There are basically two types. The drive-in screw-out and the screw-in screw-out.

The drive-in screw-out variety are quicker to arrange than the second type and for this reason are more convenient to place as running belays. However, they have a tendency to shatter hard or brittle ice and cause what's known as 'dinner plating' – a disconcerting occurrence where the ice breaks away in big

(48) Placing an ice screw. Start off with a small hole made with the pick then hammer gently and turn at the same time (a). Once the screw begins to bite, use the pick of an axe or hammer or a second screw to increase the leverage (b). Make sure it goes in to the hilt

chunks around the screw. The drive-in screw-out tubular variety are much less likely to cause this as they displace the ice up the tube.

Screw-in screw-out ice screws are a little slower to place and often require both hands to place properly. It is necessary to make a small hole to start the screw off. They are placed by turning and tapping at the same time until you feel it bite. Once it has bitten you can then use the pick of the ice axe or another screw to continue turning (Photos 48a and b). There are some makes of screw-in screw-out that are possible to fix in by turning with the hand nearly all the way. These types are distinguishable by the three or four cutting teeth at the end. Titanium screws are particularly easy to place by hand.

You must remember to clear the ice out of all tubular screws as soon as you take them out, for if the temperature is below freezing the ice will stay locked inside the tube and you won't be able to use the screw until it has melted out.

Whenever you anchor with ice screws you must try to use at least two and make sure that they are placed at least 45 cm apart (Photo 49a) so that one screw does not weaken the ice around another. If, when you are placing a screw, it reaches a point where it will not go in any further, the chances are that you will have hit rock. Don't try to force it because you may push the ice off the face or bend the screw. Any ice screw that cannot be inserted right up to the eye should be tied off with a clove hitch on the screw right up against the ice (Photo 49b).

Sometimes in hot or sunny weather, particularly when practising techniques on a glacier, ice screws conduct heat and can melt out. Try to cover them over with ice or some other suitable item of kit and this will slow the process down.

Ice Bollard

The same principles apply here as they do to the snow bollard, though of course an ice bollard does not have to be quite so large as a snow bollard. They are quite time-consuming to cut so it is

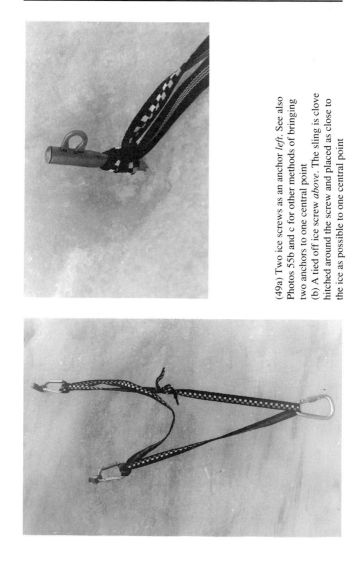

(49a) Two ice screws as an anchor *left*. See also Photos 55b and c for other methods of bringing two anchors to one central point

(b) A tied off ice screw *above*. The sling is clove hitched around the screw and placed as close to the ice as possible to one central point

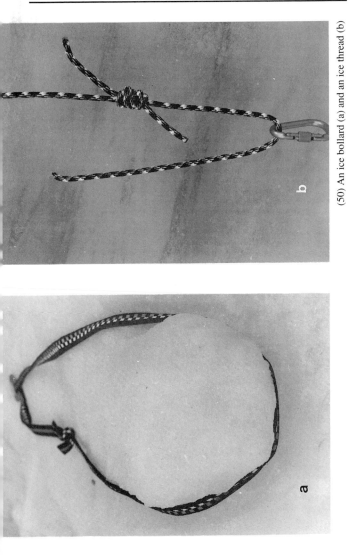

(50) An ice bollard (a) and an ice thread (b)

always better to try to look for a suitable feature to fashion one out of. This will cut the work down considerably. As they don't have to be quite so large it is sometimes possible to anchor to them via a sling around the bollard. You must ensure that there is a good lip at the back to hook the rope or sling under (Photo 50a).

Ice Thread

An effective ice thread can be achieved by making two holes in the ice with an ice screw. The holes should begin at least 25 cm apart and meet deep in the ice. The problem is of course to get the holes to meet. A sling, preferably a piece of rope because it's easier to thread, is then threaded through and the ends tied with either a double fisherman's or a ring bend. Photo 50b shows the finished product to prove that it can be done!

It is also possible to thread icicles, but only use really thick ones and even then be wary of their strength. Always put the sling around the lower part of the icicle. If using them as an anchor from which to belay you should always back them up with an ice screw or any other anchor.

Ice Tools

You can anchor yourself to an ice tool or both tools placed in the ice. You must make sure that the placements are as good as you can possibly achieve and also that the wrist loops are in a good, strong condition. When using two tools, try to bring both wrist loops to one central point and clip the two together with a single karabiner. Try to back them up with a second type of anchor, such as an ice screw for extra security.

METHODS OF TYING IN TO ANCHORS

Having described a wide variety of methods of creating anchors on the mountain, this next section looks at the options available for securing yourself in order to belay a companion.

The methods can be split in to the following categories:

1. The rope directly around the anchor or anchors
2. The rope attached to the anchor or anchors with a karabiner
3. The rope into multiple anchors brought to one central point
4. The anchor directly into the harness

We will consider each separately. Remember all the time that without exception you should always be fixed tightly to your anchor and be standing or sitting in a position that anticipates the direction of loading.

If you allow slack in the tie off to the anchor you will be jerked forward until your weight comes on to the anchor and if you are off to one side of the anticipated direction of loading, you will be pulled into line if someone falls off. A combination of the two basic errors is often disastrous. Think carefully – it is an important aspect of the safety chain.

1. The Rope Direct

The rope can be looped directly over a block or spike of rock and the end secured to the harness with a figure of eight knot tied through the central loop (Photo 51a). The rope could be secured equally well using a clove hitch into a karabiner or a figure of eight knot tied into a bight of rope and clipped via a karabiner into the central loop or tie on point. If you have more than one anchor point to tie into you must take the slack rope and repeat the process.

Using the rope to tie directly into anchors does take up a fair length of the rope and so is not commonly done. It is most useful in situations where you have run out of gear or the block or flake you want to tie around is too large for a sling.

If you are tied on with the rope directly around your waist you tie off from the anchor into the rope that goes around your waist.

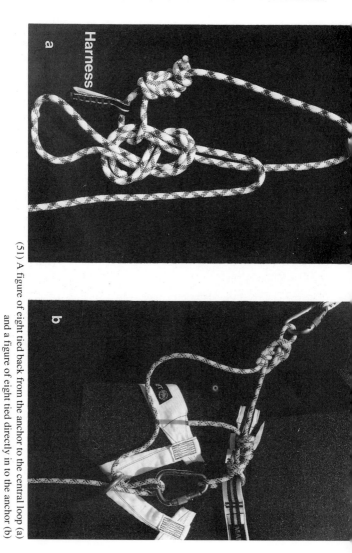

(51) A figure of eight tied back from the anchor to the central loop (a) and a figure of eight tied directly in to the anchor (b)

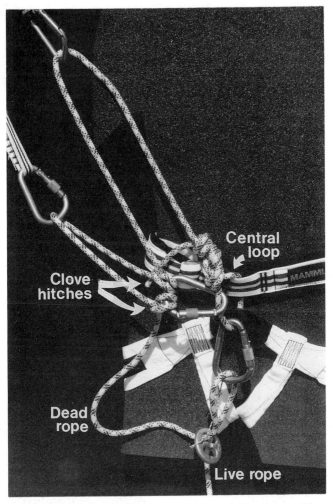

(52) Tying in to anchors – with clove hitches back to the central loop

2. The Rope through Karabiners on the Anchors

There is very little difference between this and the previous heading. However, there are one or two subtle differences that make it much easier and more versatile.

The simplest way to secure yourself to the anchor is with a figure of eight knot tied in a bight of the rope and clipped in to a screwgate karabiner on the anchor (Photo 51b). You could equally as well use a clove hitch directly into the krab. The drawback with this method is that if you have to stand out of arm's reach of your anchor, it can be difficult to gauge the correct length of the attachment in order to get tight to the anchor. My recommendation, therefore, is to only attach yourself in this way if you are within arm's reach of your anchor point. You will also find it inconvenient to attach to multiple anchors.

If you do have to move out of arm's reach of your anchor or anchor points, the system illustrated in Photo 52 will be found significantly more convenient. Take the main climbing rope and clip it into the first of the anchor krabs. Don't tie a knot, just pass it through the krab. Screw up the gate. Take the rope back to a large pear-shaped krab which is attached to the central loop and secure it with a clove hitch or figure of eight. The clove hitch is more easily adjustable. To tie into the second anchor point simply repeat the same process. You could go on *ad infinitum* like this but obviously there comes a point where it would be overkill.

If both anchors are a long way from the stance, take the rope and clip it in to the first anchor. Then run it through the krab on the central loop, from there take it through the second anchor point krab. You now have a sort of 'M' shape of ropes which act like a pulley system. Use the friction generated to lower yourself back down to the stance whereupon you secure the rope that runs through the central loop krab and the rope that ultimately goes to your partner. It may of course happen that the second anchor point is within arm's reach. In this case you can tie into it directly with a clove hitch or figure of eight (Photo 53).

(53) Tying in to anchors – the main one is clove hitched to the central loop and the second direct to the anchor

(54) Two alternatives to a screwgate karabiner

A word or two here about the use of screwgate karabiners on anchors. Whenever you attach a rope to your harness or central loop I recommend that you use a screwgate karabiner. I also recommend that you use one for your main anchor attachment. Any secondary anchors could be connected with a snaplink provided that you assure yourself that it is safe to do so. Climbers tend not to carry enormous numbers of screwgate krabs so if you do find yourself requiring the reassurance of a screwgate, and you don't have one to hand, rig up two snaplinks back to back or gates opposite as illustrated in Photo 54.

3. Multiple Anchors to One Central Point

Occasionally it may be convenient to bring two or more anchors to one central point of attachment. This can be done in a number of ways. One thing that you must remember though whenever you connect into multiple anchors is that if one anchor were to fail the load must come on to the secondary ones without any shock loading. Two anchor points can be brought together into one point if it so happens that the slings are of equal length. If they are not equal it may be possible to shorten them by tying a knot in the longest or extending the shortest.

There are three methods of using a single sling to bring anchors to a central point:

Photo 55a shows clove hitches tied at the anchor krab and the attachment point. The shock loading should one anchor fail will be negligible. It is possible to use this without the clove hitch at the central attachment point but you need to be certain that both the anchors are equally sound. This gives the advantage of being able to change your position on the stance yet maintain an equal loading on both anchors.

Photo 55b shows two anchor points brought together with a sling tied at the central attachment point with an overhand knot. If you don't tie an overhand knot and simply clip in to the doubled sling between the two anchors, you have a very dangerous and incorrect way of tying into two anchors, yet one that is com-

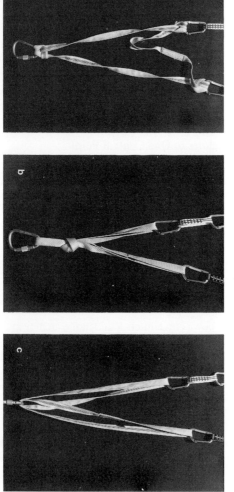

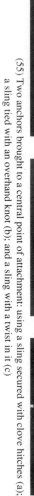

(55) Two anchors brought to a central point of attachment: using a sling secured with clove hitches (a); a sling tied with an overhand knot (b); and a sling with a twist in it (c)

monly seen. It will be immediately obvious that should one anchor fail the whole system will come undone. One often sees bolts connected in this manner, particularly on pre-rigged climbs or abseil descents. You should always rearrange the anchor more safely. What price for a life?

Photo 55c shows two anchor points brought to a central point with a twist in the sling. This is quick to rig but if one anchor fails you cannot avoid a shock loading on the other. Be sure that both anchors are equally sound.

4. Clipping in Directly to the Anchor

There is very little to be said about this method except that it is obviously very convenient should the occasion arise. You must of course be sure that the attachment is the correct length. I would also not recommend you to be too close to the anchor. For instance it would not really be practical to clip yourself in directly to a wire runner or the eye of a peg or ice screw. Let common sense prevail!

Abseiling

FIGURE OF EIGHT DESCENDEUR

Many people carry a figure of eight descendeur with them on all climbs. It is not a vital piece of kit by any means because many alternatives do exist. My feeling is that unless an item of kit has more than one function then it is probably not worth carrying. While it is true that the figure of eight can be used both for abseiling and belaying, its level of performance in the latter is a little limited. However, if you know that you have to do a lot of abseiling on your day out it may be worth taking one along.

A problem that sometimes occurs when doing multiple abseils is that the descendeur becomes too hot too handle. I'm sure that many climbers have been caught unawares a few times on hot sunny days. There's nothing that brings one back to reality quite like a scalding hot figure of eight dropping on to bare legs after pulling the rope through at the end of an abseil! Although it does become very hot there should be no danger of it melting the rope. It is generally accepted that the bulk of aluminium should dissipate the heat more efficiently than other abseiling devices.

Essentially the figure of eight is a fairly foolproof device for abseiling. There is however one point that is worthy of consideration (Photo 56). If you set up the device as shown in (a) it may happen that while you are negotiating a lip of an overhang or roof the descendeur becomes trapped against the lip and the rope flicks up over the device and the whole thing jams up (b). If this happens and you are unable to take the weight off the rope because you are hanging free, you may have a major epic on your hands. To avoid this situation occurring set it up as shown in (c). There are some devices available that have horns on the large ring which serve to prevent the larksfooting problem and so you don't have to be quite so careful in rigging them up.

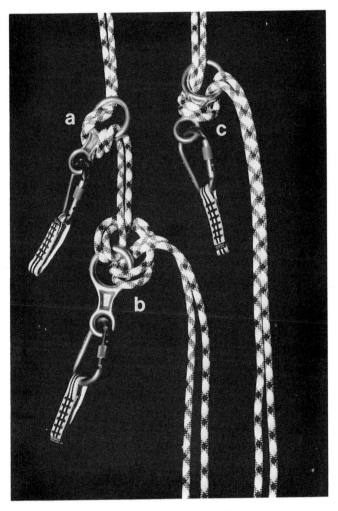

(56) The figure of eight descendeur

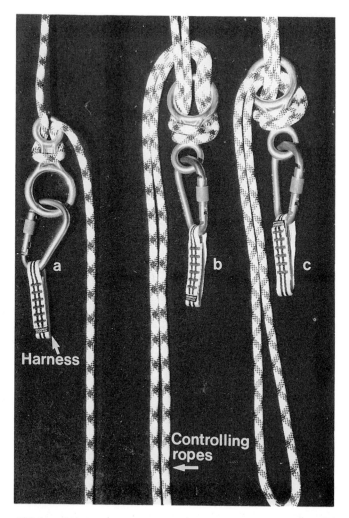

(57) (b) and (c) show a way of locking off the figure of eight

It is also possible to use the small hole of the figure of eight in the same way as the large one. Once again be particularly careful to ensure that the rope can't flick over the top (Photo 57a). This is a particularly useful method if you are abseiling on a single 9 mm rope.

Though unlikely with a figure of eight, you may find that there is not enough friction to control the speed of descent. Should this be the case simply take the controlling rope under your thigh and control the speed of descent by wrapping the rope around your leg (Photo 58a). This method works for other 'mechanical' methods of abseiling too.

The most effective way to lock off a figure of eight, or indeed any other form of mechanical abseil device, is by repeated turns of the controlling rope around the thigh or one turn around your waist. The turn around the waist is perhaps a little more efficient and safe. Turns around the thigh tend to fall down and may come completely undone. This cannot happen with the turn around the waist. Furthermore it is possible to leave the rope around your waist and feed it out gradually if you want to descend a little at a time. This will be found particularly useful in self-rescue situations (Photo 58b). Both these methods apply to most 'mechanical' methods of abseiling. A third way to lock off the figure of eight is illustrated in Photos 57b and c. This is very secure but sometimes difficult to arrange if you are unable to get just a little bit of weight off the rope.

THE BELAY PLATE

Belay plates can also be used for abseiling. Unfortunately they have a tendency to twist the ropes quite badly and can jam up at inconvenient times. Of greater significance, though, is the fact that some ropes will slide through the plate more smoothly than others. This problem can also occur if abseiling on ropes of different thicknesses. This presents a serious problem if you are abseiling on double ropes threaded around an anchor in order to

(58) Increasing the friction on descent: two more turns around the thigh will lock it off (a).
A way of increasing the friction that will also look if you let go of the controlling rope (b)

recover them afterwards. If one rope does not run as smoothly as the other it creates a certain amount of creep around the anchor and may cause the ends to become unequal in length. As you might imagine, if this occurs high on a cliff during the descent it could present a very serious situation. For 'smoother' abseiling you should connect the plate to the harness with double krabs.

A general point about abseiling worth making here is that there is always noticeably more effective friction at the start of an abseil than there is further down. On a long steep abseil you may find it difficult to get moving at first and have to actually push the rope through the device. Nearer the end of the descent it may be all that you can do to hang on to the rope. Though not always practical you should consider using leather gloves for abseiling.

THE ITALIAN HITCH

This is a suitable method of abseiling but subject to the limitations discussed on page 22.

KARABINER BRAKES

Probably the most versatile abseil device. Setting up a karabiner brake requires no more equipment than the climber would normally carry. Though it is preferable and safer to set up with screwgate krabs it can also be set up using snaplinks. With practice it is possible to set the brake up to generate as much or as little friction as is required.

There are a number of different ways to set up a krab brake. Whichever set-up you use it is important to ensure that under no circumstances will the rope rub on the gate of a krab and cause it to open accidentally. Photo 59 shows a straightforward way to set up the brake and also a simple yet very effective way of increasing the friction and ultimately the control. It is very easy to overkill on the friction to such an extent that you may be

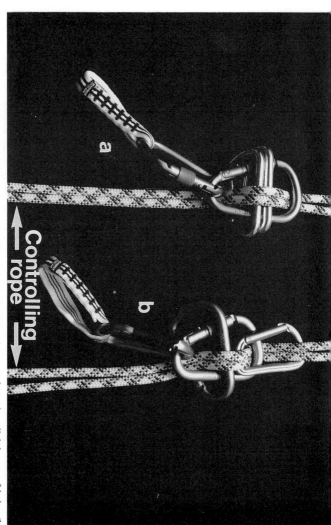

(59) The karabiner brake: a simple two bar brake (a) and a way of creating slightly more friction (b)

unable to move! This is particularly the case if using double 11 mm ropes. In 'normal' circumstances the number of krabs used in the set-up illustrated is sufficient. The only time one may need more friction is after Christmas lunch or when lowering two people at the same time such as in improvised rescue.

It is really only worth using karabiner brakes with double rope. It requires a great many krabs to set up enough friction with a single rope. A word of warning – the krab brake is quite complicated to set up and can be set up dangerously, so be sure you practise it well before putting it to the test in a real situation. You would be well advised to use similar krabs throughout the brake as this makes operation much smoother. Make sure that the krab that supports the bar krabs is fairly large. If it is much smaller than the bar krabs the brake can slip off if, for some reason, you take your weight off the rope. They don't become completely detached but will give you a nasty shock when you put your weight back on the abseil rope. There have been many climbers who have discovered the folly of pulling the rope through the brake at the end of the abseil only to find the brake bar krabs go tumbling away – fun on sea cliffs. It is worth considering that if you do use karabiner brakes each time you abseil, modern lightweight karabiners are prone to damage by dirty or gritty ropes. This can cause an excessive amount of wear on the krab, weakening it to no small degree.

PITON BAR BRAKES

This simple but effective device can be set up using a karabiner and an angle piton. It is very quick to set up and it is possible to generate more friction by adding a karabiner in the same way as that used on a karabiner brake (Photo 60). Be careful to ensure that the piton has no rough edges that may damage the rope. This method of abseiling would be most appropriate to winter or Alpine climbing where one would normally carry a few pitons.

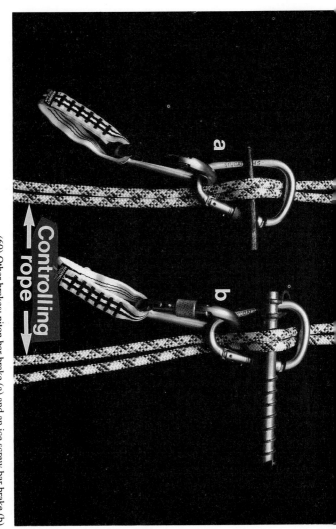

(60) Other brakes: piton bar brake (a) and an ice screw bar brake (b)

THE ABSEIL RACK

A large and cumbersome device more appropriate to caving than climbing but nevertheless one that merits consideration in situations of Outdoor Centre 'production line' abseiling. It is less destructive to ropes and one can generate as much or as little friction as required by adjusting the distance between the bars and the number of bars used.

'CLASSIC' METHODS OF ABSEILING

There are a number of methods of 'classic' abseiling, all of which require the rope to be wrapped around some part of the body in order to create enough friction to control the speed of descent. My feeling is that all of these methods should only be used in emergencies – situations where no technical equipment other than a rope is available.

The proper classic abseil is rigged by standing astride the ropes facing the anchor point. Reach down with your right hand and bring the rope up behind your right thigh, across your chest, over your left shoulder and back into your right hand. The friction is controlled by bringing the right hand round your front for more friction and away from you for less.

Another form of classic abseil is to make up a Dulfer seat harness and take the abseil rope up through the karabiner, over the left shoulder and across the back into the right hand. This generates little friction and is also dangerous as clothing can get trapped in the karabiner.

Note: if you are left-handed please read left for right and right for left.

You should not really use any of these methods of abseiling on a single rope and neither can you use the safety back-up method of holding the end of the rope to stop someone in difficulty (see Abseil Safety below).

When using the 'proper' classic abseil you will find it more comfortable to twist sideways and lead with the right foot (left for left-handers). This is particularly important when stepping down over obstacles as leading with the other foot may cause the rope to ride up around the knee, causing you to flip upside down.

ABSEIL SAFETY

Sadly, there have been some tragic abseiling accidents over the years. Some may reasonably be attributed to fate while others to errors of judgement. Truth to tell, abseiling is a very simple and straightforward exercise but it is this simplicity that leads to a complacent attitude and accidents.

Always check the abseil anchor thoroughly. Don't trust old decayed slings or in situ pegs or nuts if you are the slightest bit suspicious of them. It is cheaper to sacrifice a bit of gear rather than a life.

Simple safety precautions like tying a knot in the end of the ropes if you know or aren't sure that they reach the ground. It is also possible to rig a very simple 'safety back-up' system while abseiling. This is best effected by putting a French prusik (page 48) on the ropes above the abseil device. The prusik is then attached to the harness with a sling. As you abseil you simply keep one hand on the rope above the French prusik and slide it down with you. If you let go of it for whatever reason it should jam and halt further descent. It is vitally important to ensure that when the load is applied to the prusik that it does not stretch out of arm's reach. If it does then you will find it very difficult to release it again. The best gauge for the length of the attachment is for the prusik to be a slightly bent arm's length away from you when the sling comes tight. I would not recommend the use of any other prusik knot for this purpose. Many of them would jam solid and the only way to release it would be to cut it with a knife. The French prusik is the only one that can still be relied upon to be released even under load.

Another form of abseil safety is to hold the the bottom of the abseil ropes whilst someone is descending. If the abseiler loses control during the descent the person at the bottom should pull the rope very hard. This will halt any further descent until the tension is released. I have seen this used to great effect on a number of occasions which would have otherwise resulted in serious injury. Please note that 'classic' methods of abseiling do not respond to this method of safety. Indeed it would be down-right dangerous to even contemplate this.

If you are the first person down the abseil and you have perhaps had to pendule or move slightly to the side of the natural hang of the ropes, it may be worth considering fixing the ropes to the anchor for safety and to make life easier for the next person to descend.

To facilitate the separation and recovery of abseil ropes it is often worthwhile to clip a short sling and krab on to one of the ropes and the other end of the sling to your harness. If you do this at the beginning of the descent it will keep the ropes separated all the way to the bottom. Furthermore if you put it on the rope that you have to pull to retrieve the abseil ropes, it serves as a reminder of the correct rope to pull. It is becoming quite common practice to use a figure of eight knot for joining two ropes together for abseiling. Through long habit the thought is slightly off-putting but there is a tremendous advantage. If you join the two ropes in this way when you come to retrieve the ropes after the abseil the knot presents a flat profile to the edge that it may be dragged over. There is therefore much less chance that the knot could jam during retrieval.

If you are unfortunate enough to get your ropes jammed, be particularly careful how you go about freeing them. Don't ever for instance, attempt to climb up a single jammed rope if it is avoidable. It may not be as jammed as it first appears.

ABSEILING PAST A KNOT

There are really very few occasions when it is necessary to join ropes together to add to the length it is possible to abseil. However, for the odd occasion where it may be necessary to abseil past a knot it is certainly a useful thing to know about.

It is possible to abseil straight over a knot in a single 9 mm rope, if you are using a figure of eight descendeur. If you are hanging free it can be difficult to feed the knot through the device but this problem can be overcome to a certain extent by having long 'tails' on the joining knot which lead the knot into the device more evenly. I would venture to suggest that you only abseil on single 9 mm rope as a last resort because there is very little friction and it can be difficult to hold such a thin rope.

If using a karabiner brake or a belay plate the situation is very different as the knot won't pass through the device. If there is a convenient ledge which coincides with the knot then simply abseil to the ledge, put in some protection for yourself whilst you take the rope out of the device and reconnect it below the knot.

Abseiling past a knot while hanging free or with no convenient ledge to stand on presents different problems. These are by no means complicated or insurmountable but will require practice in a safe and controlled situation.

If you know that you have to abseil past a knot before you set off, rig a safety back up French prusik as previously described. It is important to connect the French prusik to the harness with its own screwgate karabiner and in such a way that the abseil device can easily be removed whilst hanging from the French prusik.

Abseil down until the joining knot is 25-30 cm away from the device (Photo 61a). This must coincide with your full weight coming on to the French prusik. Take the abseil rope out of the device and put it back on below the knot (Photo 61b), then make sure that the joining knot sits up against the device. Lock off the device securely; reach up and put one hand on the rope above the French prusik. By pulling down smoothly but firmly on top of the prusik it will release and your weight will come back on to the abseil device. Once your weight is back on the device

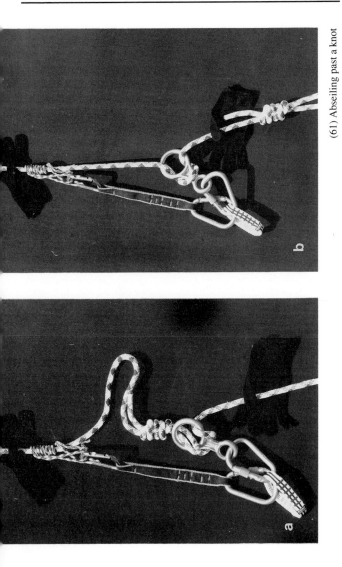

(61) Abseiling past a knot

disconnect and release the French prusik. Unless you have a second knot to pass, it is probably not worth putting it back on, though you may want it for a safety back-up. Using this system it is possible to abseil past a knot in less than 30 seconds, not the usual 30 minutes as is often seen!

Please note that proper preparation is vital to smoothness and safety. The length of the French prusik and the distance you stop above the knot are both crucial. On no account should you let the prusik go out of arm's reach and neither should you allow the knot to come closer than 25 cm before your full weight is taken on the prusik. This system can also be used if you are lowering someone on two ropes joined together and need to pass the knot through the lowering device. The same principles of safety and technique apply, though it would be true to say that the length of the French prusik is not quite so critical (see page 73) – provided it is not too short!

Ascending a Fixed Rope

There are few occasions in normal day to day climbing that require the ability to ascend a fixed rope. Situations where you might have to do so include emergency situations such as during the rescue of an injured climber or escaping from a crevasse; on a 'Big Wall' route where the second often climbs the rope for speed or for seconding artificial climbs. A mechanical ascending device is also used as a method of safeguarding yourself on long mountaineering routes where fixed ropes are left in place to assist with rapid ascent and descent of the mountain. Though in that situation the rope rarely bears the full weight of the climber.

The techniques can be broadly categorized into methods that employ a mechanical device, such as a Jumar and those that rely on loops of cord, such as the prusik knot, wrapped around the rope. By coincidence the two techniques are popularly called 'Jumaring' (using any mechanical device) and 'Prusiking' (when using a knotted loop). The first category is by far the most efficient and the second although less so is the best that can be done in an emergency situation.

Whichever you choose to use the basic technique of ascent is the same. A long sling or loop is used for the foot and a shorter one attached to the harness. These two slings or loops are more than adequate and there is no need to resort to using three loops as people have done in years gone by. The sit harness loop is connected *above* the foot loop. It is possible to do it the other way around but the margins of safety are less and it is more awkward to work. The ideal length of each loop can only be determined by practice and is ultimately dependent on the size and agility of the individual.

As a rough guide to the length of the sit harness loop, put a prusik knot on the rope and attach it to the harness via a karabiner. The prusik knot itself should be at about forehead-level when you are hanging in your harness and the loop is tight. The length of the foot loop is best determined by hanging from the sit loop with a prusik knot on the rope. Put your foot in the bottom of the loop and bend your leg to the point where you feel you could most comfortably stand up from (Photo 62). The efficiency with which you prusik is measured by the amount of height you gain when you stand up straight in the foot loop each time. If you can bend your leg behind your ear and still stand up on it then you will probably have reached the maximum efficiency. The same principles apply to determining the length of sling for a mechanical device.

Movement up the rope is effected by standing straight legged in the foot loop and moving the sit loop up. It is an energetic and quite tiring process to ascend a rope in such a manner, so be prepared to huff and puff a bit. It is very important to try to conserve energy, particularly if you have a long way to go. When you try to stand in the foot loop, make sure that you do so by pushing with your leg directly underneath you. Have the rope running up your chest all the time. Try to avoid hanging out backwards and having to pull yourself up with your arms. You will also find it easier if your foot loop is larksfooted around your foot to prevent it slipping out. If one leg gets tired of doing all the work simply swap feet or even use both feet in the loop.

If you have a chest harness on it is worth considering clipping the rope through a karabiner attached to the chest harness. This helps to keep you close in to the rope. You can also clip in the foot loop to the harness though unless you are using a system where the foot loop is fixed above the sit loop, this can be more trouble than it is worth.

For reasons of safety it is advisable that you consider tying a figure of eight knot at 5 m intervals as an extra back up. This knot can then be clipped into the central loop of your harness so that if for some reason the prusiks or devices should fail you do at least have something to stop you falling off the rope.

If you have a large or heavy rucksack on your back it is well worth taking it off and putting it on the rope below you. This acts as a weight to hold the ropes taut and actually makes it easier to move the loops or devices up the rope.

(62) Ascending a fixed rope: using prusik loops (a) and mechanical devices (b)

(63) The foot hitch for ascending a fixed rope

For relevant knots to use for prusiking refer to the section on 'prusik' knots (page 44).

IMPROVISED ASCENT METHODS

If you find yourself with only one prusik loop it is quite possible to improvise in a number of ways and the following methods work well.

Put the prusik on the rope and attach it to your sit harness. Sit back in it and lift your foot to the point from where you can most comfortably stand up. Wrap the rope a few times around your foot, hold the slack and loaded ropes together and stand up. Still standing, move the sit loop up until it is tight, sit back and repeat the procedure. Photo 63 shows a foot hitch alternative to the wrap around the foot. Make sure that you tie a figure of eight in the rope every 2 m or so and clip it back into the harness as a safety back-up.

A second method which is less tiring but potentially quite dangerous is to use a belay plate and prusik. The belay plate is attached to the harness and the prusik used as a foot loop above the belay plate. Slide the foot loop up as high as possible and stand up. At the same time, pull the rope through the plate. When standing at your maximum height, lock off the plate and sit back in your harness. *Beware!* If you let go of the controlling rope of the belay plate you will head earthwards very quickly. With that in mind, tie off back to the harness with a figure of eight knot more frequently than the other methods described. You could use the Alpine clutch in place of the belay plate. This is very much safer because you can arrange it so that you are only able to pull the rope through as you stand up. If you let go of it , it should jam up. The only disadvantage with this is that if, for some reason, you need to go back down the rope, it isn't possible without having to rearrange the whole set up.

Escaping from the System

This is the term used to describe the technique of releasing oneself from the belay system and end of rope whilst ensuring the security of the climber you are responsible for, usually with their full weight hanging on the rope.

The reasons for having to 'escape' are too numerous to mention them all but an example might be that you are belaying your partner when a large rock is dislodged by a party above and renders him or her unconscious. Another typical example would be on a glacier where a member of the party falls into a crevasse. Whatever the reason for having to escape and help your partner you must initially overcome the problem of having their full weight hanging from you and being tied in to the anchors.

In the first instance it is important to establish the need to escape while the person is hanging on the rope. It may be possible to lower the victim down to a ledge or even to the ground before you escape. If that be the case many of your problems are instantly solved. And don't isolate yourself in your predicament, there may be other people around who are more than willing to assist.

THE BASIC PROCEDURE

Whether practising or doing it for real, make sure that you can see a way out of the situation the whole time – always think 'what will happen if…?' Work logically and safely, and try to keep things as simple, as tidy and as straightforward as possible.

The sequence of photographs shows how to escape from the system most efficiently in the easiest of all situations – one anchor point within arm's reach (Photos 64, 65 and 66).

Proceed as follows. Tie off the belay plate; put a French prusik on the load rope and clip it back into the anchor (extend it with slings if it is not long enough). Slide the prusik forward until it is under tension but make sure that it remains within arm's

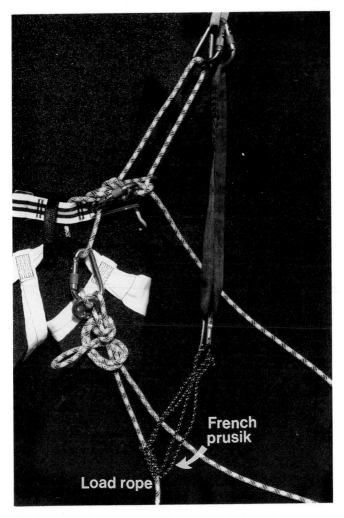

(64) Escaping from the system – stage one

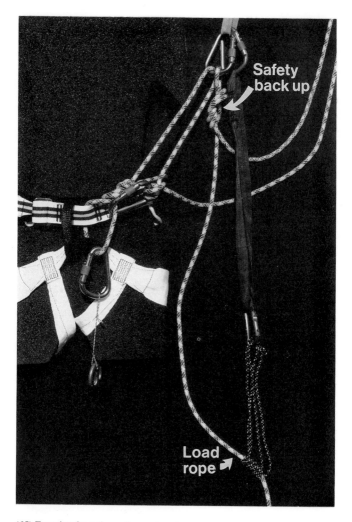

(65) Escaping from the system – stage two

(66) Escaping from the system – stage three

reach. Release the belay plate and gradually lower the weight on to the French prusik. All the weight should now be directly on the anchor point. Take the rope out of the belay plate and fix it back to the anchor with a figure of eight knot and separate krab (ensure that there is a little slack in the rope to allow for slippage and to facilitate unclipping later on). Untie yourself from the anchor making sure you clip into an alternative anchor for your own safety. Mind you don't drop your belay plate! Finally consider backing up your anchor as necessary.

It is worth noting that with some harnesses, mainly ones with a separate belt and leg loops, it is possible to escape by simply tying off the belay plate, undoing the harness and pulling it through the central loop. Some of these two-piece harnesses have little tabs through which the manufacturer recommends you to thread the rope when tying on. These tabs are purely to stop the rope sliding around in the harness but are not absolutely necessary and are certainly not load-bearing. If you do thread the rope through the tabs you will need to go through the longer process of escaping the system.

Having escaped, you are now free to move around at your leisure. You may have to descend to the person hanging on the other end of the rope, in which case use all the spare rope to abseil down on. If you are happy to abseil off the same anchor that your victim is hanging on then simply abseil off the rope on the other side of the figure of eight knot in Photo 66. If you are not happy to do this then you should rig another anchor for your abseil. For safety you should tie a knot in the end of the rope and use a French prusik safety back-up.

DEALING WITH PROBLEMS

Inevitably problems will crop up. The most likely one to occur is that you are unable to reach the anchor point from your stance when doing the escape and before you can escape you must create a 'new anchor point'. To do this tie a prusik loop or a klemheist in a tape sling around both ropes going back to the anchor. Whichever knot you decide to use put in as many turns as you can. Do this as far back as you can comfortably reach (Photo 67) and clip in a karabiner. You now use this krab as your new anchor point and escape in the same way as described previously. It is very important that, once you have untied from the end of the rope, you tie knots that will prevent the new anchor from sliding off the end (Photo 68).

You may find yourself with two or even three anchors, each tied into separately with the rope. If it is possible, link all or a selection of the ropes together when tying the klemheist or prusik as described and use this as your new anchor. If this is not possible then you must put a klemheist or a prusik around each of the anchor ropes and link them together until they form one central anchor point. Remember that once you have escaped you will be in a position to back everything up as you see necessary.

It is of course terribly easy to get yourself into an awful tangle when escaping so you should practise in a controlled situation as much as possible before having to put it to the real test. It is a good idea to present yourself with situations to deal with on low-level practice crags – you can make them as simple or as ludicrously difficult as you like! For instance, if you are using a single rope and the victim is more than half the rope's length below you you will not have enough rope to reach him or her by abseil. In this case you must abseil down as far as you can and then transfer yourself on to the victim's rope and continue down by prusiking.

If you are climbing on double ropes or you have a spare rope, as you may do when travelling across a glacier, you would be advised to only tie off one rope when doing your escape. Although the other end may be tied into the victim, you will at least be able to use the full length as there will not be any tension in it. Once you get to the victim you can untie him or her from it completely thus giving yourself greater flexibility in coping with the situation.

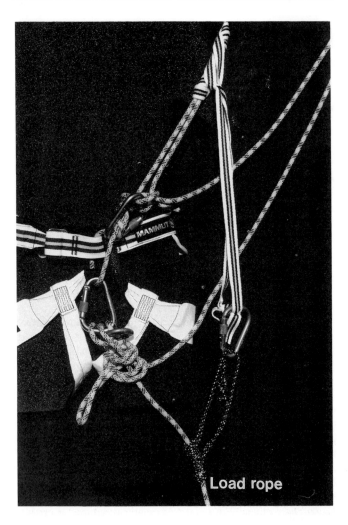

Load rope

(67) Escaping the system when the anchor point is out of reach – stage one

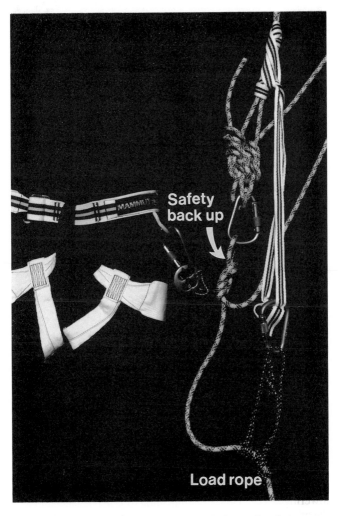

(68) Escaping the system when the anchor point is out of reach – stage two

There are almost certain to be running belays on the rope between you and the victim. You must decide what to do with them – leave them in or take them out – as you descend. So much depends on the situation that it is impossible to suggest a standard procedure. However, if by removing a running belay you are likely to cause the victim to move from their position, I would suggest that you leave it in.

AFTER THE ESCAPE

Having escaped and gone down to your victim you may have to administer first aid and also rig him or her in some kind of full body harness for comfort. You must then decide what to do from this point onwards. What you do is obviously dependent on innumerable factors but your choice can be limited to four main courses of action:

1.   Return to the stance and lower the victim to the ground either in one go or in stages

2.   Return to the stance and hoist the victim to the same stance or to safety

3.   Leave the victim in situ while you go for help

4.   Evacuate yourself and the victim simultaneously (assisted evacuation)

Lowering the Victim

Once you have decided to lower the victim we will assume that you have regained the stance and everything is set up and ready to go as in Photos 66 or 68. To convert the system to a lower, unclip the figure of eight and put the rope in an appropriate lowering device. Hold the controlling rope in one hand and with the other release the French prusik. The load should come on to lowering device as gradually as possible. Continue lowering with one hand keeping the French prusik, now an autobloc, released with the other. If you want to stop lowering and let go of the ropes for any reason the load should be taken by the autobloc. If you need to leave the system unattended for any length of time you should tie off the belay device in the appropriate manner.

If you can lower the victim to the ground in one go you are fortunate and should do so! To get yourself down you should tie off the lowering rope as soon as the victim reaches the ground. Have a little slack in the rope so that you can abseil down. It is really not worth messing around trying to retrieve rope and gear unless you need it to continue to civilization. You can always come back and collect it later – it might still be there! If you do not have enough rope to reach the ground in one lower then you must obviously do it in stages. This will be limited to a maximum of 22-25 m if you are climbing on a single rope and so can be very time consuming indeed.

The lower of each stage is fairly straightforward if you can trust your victim to rig a safe anchor for him or herself at the end of each lower. Proceed as follows. Lower the victim to a convenient stopping place or just under the halfway mark on the rope. Get them to rig an anchor and clip in securely. *They must not untie from the end of the rope.* Take the rope out of the lowering device and pass it through the abseil anchor and abseil on the double rope so that you can recover it once you reach the victim. Remember that at all times you must look to your own safety as well as that of the victim. On the abseil it is worth using a safety back-up.

Now let us consider what to do if you do not trust the victim or the victim is unable to rig a safe anchor at the end of each lower. Take the rope out of the the lowering device but leave the victim protected by the autobloc which remains attached to the anchor. Clip the rope through a krab on the anchor and throw the remaining slack, with a knot tied in the end, down the cliff. Put an abseiling device, preferably a belay plate, on the doubled rope for yourself and a safety back up. Untie the original autobloc which was left on to protect the victim and set off down. As you abseil the victim is protected by the fact that their rope passes around the abseil anchor, through your safety back-up and through the abseil device. The use of the belay plate makes this a safer device to use. In theory, if the victim were to roll off the ledge he or she should not fall too far. Once you reach the victim you should of course put in an anchor and before doing anything else clip yourselves into it. Retrieve your ropes and the procedure can be repeated all the way down the cliff or until you reach safety.

There are of course all sorts of variations to the techniques but having practised and mastered the basics you will soon learn what they are. Remember it is important to keep things as simple and as straightforward as possible.

HOISTING

There are two basic types of hoist used in rescue situations: the assisted hoist and the unassisted hoist. Before undertaking a hoist in a rescue situation you should be absolutely certain that this is what you need to do. If your victim is a 'dead' weight on the end of the rope it is often impossible for one person to hoist efficiently.

Assisted Hoist

This hoist is by far the simplest to rig up and the most effective in use. It is particularly useful in a situation where your second is unable to climb a section of the route or has fallen off to one side and cannot get back on again. It can however be difficult for the victim to assist if he or she is hanging in space. It can be rigged very quickly and does not even require you to escape from the system if you are using any belaying device other than a body belay.

Proceed as follows. Tie off the belay device. Put an autobloc on the load rope and clip it back into the central loop on your harness. Make this attachment quite short, certainly no more than 30 cm from the device as you do not want it to slide down the rope and out of arm's reach. The load should now be predominantly on the anchor. Take up some slack rope and throw a loop with a krab clipped in to it down to the victim. Tell the victim to clip the krab into the central loop of their harness. Make sure that the rope is not twisted. Untie the belay plate and lower the victim's weight on to the autobloc.

You are now ready to hoist. The victim should pull on the rope that travels towards him or her. This is easy to establish – neither the victim nor the rescuer pulls on the rope that is tied to the victim and has the autobloc on it (load rope) and of the remaining two one of them comes down to the victim and the other back up to the belayer (Photo 69). Both the rescuer and the victim pull simultaneously and if the victim can walk up the crag or the slope it can be a simple matter to hoist them up. Should either of you need to rest at any time simply lower the weight on to the autobloc and let go with all hands. This is an ideal way to get over the crux moves of the climb!

Once you have hoisted far enough you will need to get back into the belaying mode again. This is simple enough to achieve but just remember to safeguard the victim before you sort everything out. This can be done most effectively by tying off the belay device.

Problems can occur with the system, especially if your victim is more than a third of the rope's length below you as the system requires three lengths of rope between rescuer and victim. Its use is also limited to situations where you are able to get a loop to the victim in the first instance. Communication is very important particularly if the victim does not understand how the system works. You must be able to converse without fear of the instructions being misinterpreted.

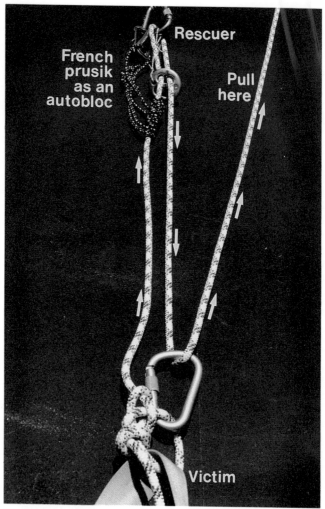

(69) The assisted hoist

Unassisted Hoists

If you are unfortunate enough to find yourself in a situation where you have no option but to hoist your victim to a safe place then you are going to require patience, muscle power, plenty of space and lots of time. It would also be to your advantage to have a few pulleys around. This is possible in glacial travel but unlikely in a crag climbing situation. Do not underestimate the difficulties involved in hoisting someone without assistance. What is essentially a simple system to set up is extraordinarily difficult to effect.

There are a number of ways of hoisting. It might even be possible, if you're very strong and the victim light, to hoist by simply pulling your victim up hand over hand. If you do do this be sure to have some kind of safety back-up for when you need to rest or if you let go of the rope. A safer way of pulling someone up directly is shown in Photo 70. A prusik is attached to the load rope and then to the rescuer's harness, but keep it quite short. The load rope is then passed through an Italian hitch at the anchor and an autobloc to the load rope. The rescuer slides the prusik down the load rope as far as it will go and uses the powerful leg muscles to do the pulling while at the same time pulling the rope through the Italian hitch. To gain a rest the load is taken by the autobloc. This system is only effective if the rescuer has the strength to lift the victim but adaptations of the technique can be used in 'pulley' hoists, as will be seen later.

A brief word here about the mechanical advantage of the different systems. The hoisting systems we use in improvised rescue do not generally use pulleys at each turn of the rope so that a rope running over a single karabiner often creates so much friction that it negates the mechanical advantage gained. One rapidly approaches the point in attempting to increase mechanical advantage where there are so many 'pulleys' in the system that it is impossible to pull the rope through! By doubling up the karabiners at each turn you reduce the angle that the rope goes through and also the friction generated. Using lightweight

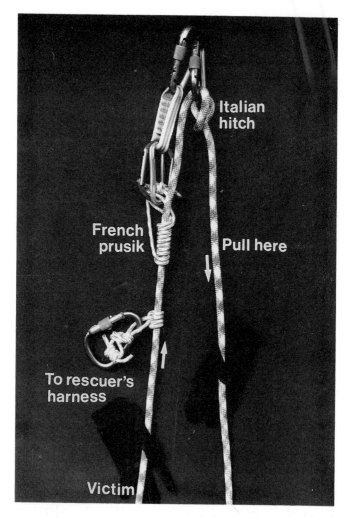

(70) The direct hoist

(71) The basic Z pulley

pulleys designed specifically for mountaineering reduces the
friction generated and increases the effects of mechanical advantage. But it's another item of gear to carry.

An additional point worth mentioning is that in using
climbing ropes much of the energy expended pulling someone
up is used in taking the stretch out of the rope.

There are so many factors that go against hoisting that it is
important to establish that it is really necessary before you begin.

The Z Pulley System

The Z pulley system or the 'two in one hoist' as it is sometimes
called is a good basic hoist to begin with and works well if there
are plenty of helpers and plenty of room to manoeuvre.

Let us assume that you are on a stance and have decided to
hoist. The set up is similar to that in Photo 66 or 68 having just
escaped from the system. Take a spare prusik loop and put it on
the load rope as far down as you can safely reach. Untie the figure
of eight knot and pass it through a new karabiner or a pulley on
the anchor, and then down through the prusik you have just put
on (Photo 71). It is to your advantage to make this latter prusik
connection as short as possible.

All the victim's weight should be hanging on the original
French prusik which is now transformed into an autobloc. To
hoist the victim you should pull on the rope that comes up from
the prusik loop. Photo 71 shows direction of rope travel and
where to pull. If the victim is able to 'walk' up the cliff then you
should ask them to do so. You will probably find that it is only
possible to move the victim a little at a time and so in between
pulls rest by lowering the weight on to the autobloc. Eventually
the prusik knot will come up to meet the autobloc. At this point
take the load on the autobloc and slide the prusik back down as
far as you can safely reach. Repeat the procedure until you are
completely exhausted or the victim is where you want him or her
to be.

If you have enough space then you can attach the pulling

rope to your harness with a belay plate or Italian hitch and use your leg muscles to pull rather than your arms. This is much less tiring. Pulling is effected by locking off the device and pulling in that position. Once you reach the limit of pull lower the victim on to the autobloc and move back down to the edge taking the slack rope in as you go.

Improved Z Pulley

To be truthful, the system previously described is very difficult to put into practice in a less than perfect situation, particularly when you have no other assistance. It is possible to improve the system slightly by a number of variants and I have found the following to be satisfactory.

Leave the system set up as before and on the pulling rope place a short prusik loop and karabiner. Tie the other end of the climbing rope into the anchor with a figure of eight knot. Bring some of the rope down to the new prusik and clip it through the krab (Photo 72a). You now have a new pulling rope and should find the whole set up much easier to pull yet you have only introduced one extra point of friction. If space is limited and it is easier for you to pull the rope downwards rather than up, rig up the new system so that the end of the rope clips in to the second prusik and you pull through the karabiner on the anchor (Photo 72b).

This system is much more efficient than the basic hoist, the only disadvantage being that you have to move the prusiks down the rope more frequently. However, the extra ease of pulling far outweighs this.

The Yosemite Lift

This type of hoist was originally developed for sack hauling on the Big Walls of Yosemite in California, USA. It is still a widely used system for that purpose but has little to recommend it for hoisting people. It works most efficiently when the anchor points

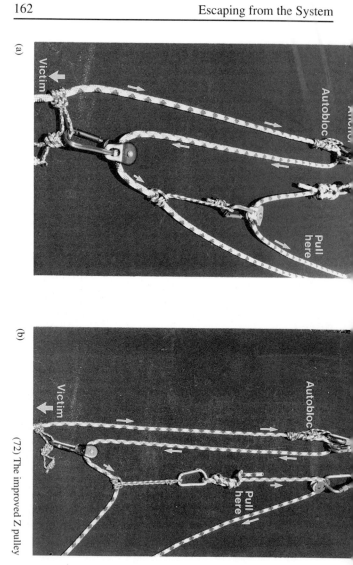

(a)

(b)

(72) The improved Z pulley

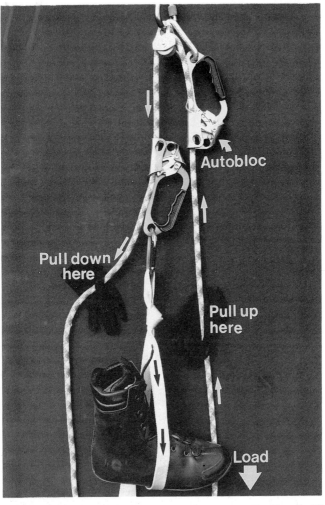

Autobloc

Pull down here

Pull up here

Load

(73) The Yosemite lift

are above you.

When climbing multi-day climbs such as those found in Yosemite, it is quite likely that you will have mechanical ascending devices with you and these can be used in place of prusik loops to make life a little easier. Photo 73 shows the basic set up. It is well worth carrying the pulley for just this purpose if you go on a climb knowing that you will have to sack haul.

The autobloc is provided by a mechanical device placed upside down on the load rope. The load rope is then passed through a pulley in the anchor and a second mechanical device placed the right way up, with a short foot loop attached, on the pulling rope. As you push down on the pulling rope with your foot you should try to pull up the load rope with the other hand.

ASSISTED EVACUATION

One day you may find yourself in a situation where you have no option but to evacuate both yourself and an injured victim who is unable to assist in any useful way. The 'traditional' way to do this has been to use an improvised rope Tragsitz. In truth, to the climber or mountaineer with limited resources it is not a feasible system of evacuation. There are a number of reasons for this, not least that it requires an extra rope, which is in itself an unlikely luxury. It is very difficult indeed to get someone on your back if you do not have anyone else to help you; it requires a good large ledge to work from each time; if any problems arise they are difficult to deal with; if the victim requires medical attention during the descent you have to stop, get him off your back, then back on... It is hardly a practical method.

The system I prefer to use is basically one in which both the rescuer and the victim abseil together from the same device, with the rescuer doing all the controlling. In this position the rescuer is allowed full flexibility and can carry the victim in the position that is most practical and comfortable. It is even possible to change positions as often as you wish on the way down. You can have the victim in front of you, by your side walking down with you, behind you, across your lap, between your legs or even below you. There are no hard and fast rules to apply to what position the victim should be in, and so much has to be left to the judgement of the rescuer. The following guidelines may be of some help in deciding as to which position is most suitable.

1. Very steep cliff/unconscious victim – across the rescuer's lap or hanging below. If you choose to have the victim hanging below, you must be very careful to ensure that you don't cause any further injury with your feet (Photo 74).

2. Slabby terrain/unconscious victim – between the rescuers legs with the victim's legs pointing out from the crag (Photo 75).

3. Any terrain/walking victim – side by side (Photo 76).

Whichever of the possible positions you decide to use the method of rigging the system is essentially the same. There is only one important variable to consider and that is the length of the sling attachment for both the victim and the rescuer to the descending device. For example, if the victim is to be across the rescuer's lap the victim's attachment must be shorter than the rescuer's. If both are to descend side by side then they must obviously be of equal length. Photos 77a and b show the simplified set up for both of these positions.

It is possible to rig an adjustable length attachment for both rescuer and victim or for one of them only. This requires extra equipment in the form of a length of 5 or 6 mm cord for each attachment so may not be practical for most situations. A cowstail with a number of possible attachments is much more versatile.

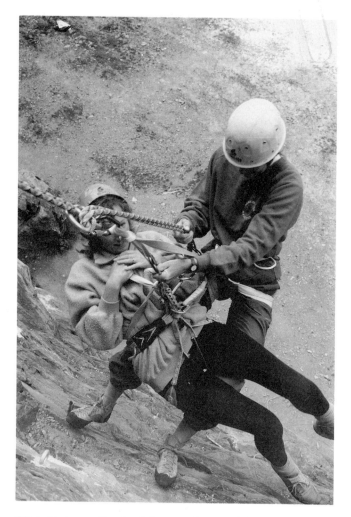

(74) Assisted evacuation: the victim across the rescuer's lap

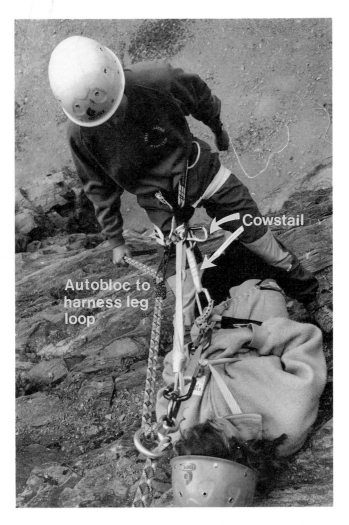

(75) Assisted evacuation: the victim between the rescuer's legs

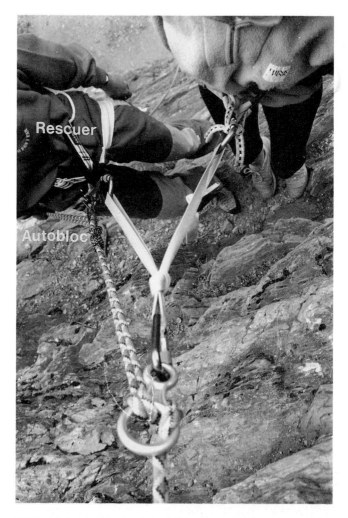

(76) Assisted evacuation: the victim and the rescuer side by side

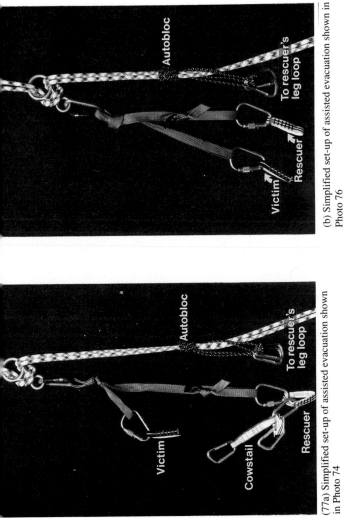

(77a) Simplified set-up of assisted evacuation shown in Photo 74

(b) Simplified set-up of assisted evacuation shown in Photo 76

THE DESCENT

The abseil device that you choose to use must generate sufficient friction to enable the rescuer to control the speed of descent of two people safely and effectively. A figure of eight abseil device or a belay plate is ideal. So also is a karabiner brake with extra friction bars. The Italian hitch generates enough friction but tends to twist the ropes and cause tangles, which is really the last thing you need to happen.

As with all these rescue situations, it is of vital importance to have some kind of fail safe system for extra security. The usual method of protecting an abseil, with the French prusik above the abseil device, is not suitable here because the device will almost certainly be beyond arm's length. Remember that the safety back up has to be well within reach. The alternative is to put the French prusik below the device and attach it to the rescuer's harness leg loop. Photo 75 shows this clearly. Lowering is then effected by the rescuer releasing the French prusik and allowing the rope to slide at the same time. If the rescuer lets go of the rope for any reason further descent will be halted as the French prusik comes tight. This method gives excellent fine control of the lower.

One minor disadvantage, and one that you need to be aware of, is that if the rescuer has let go with both hands to attend to something else, any movement upwards of the leg that has the French prusik attached will cause some rope to slide through the device. This is by no means a major problem but it is as well to be aware that it might happen.

You could attach the safety back-up French prusik to the front of the rescuer's harness. If you have the inclination it is worth trying in a practice situation but it is definitely not as effective as having it attached to your leg loop.

As you descend you will probably find it easier to have one hand on the victim's harness and the other on the controlling rope. If you need to pull the victim away from the crag, perhaps to lie across your lap or between your legs, use a cowstail to hold them in close to you. This should be clipped to the victim at the harness attachment point and to the rescuer anywhere on the harness that is convenient and comfortable. By pushing out from the cliff face with your legs you will find with relatively little effort it is possible to keep the victim away from the rock.

The ropes are rigged through the anchor in the same way as you would for a 'normal' abseil retreat from a climb and you descend on both ropes together. Thus, with single rope you are limited to 22-25 m abseils but with two ropes the full length of each rope. The ropes can be pulled down after each stage, making sure that you secure both you and your victim to the mountain first. Don't worry about leaving gear behind – it is much more important to get you and your victim down without any problems occurring.

An Alternative Method

The above system works very well and is versatile enough to cope with any situation you may find yourself in but it may be of interest to try out a slight variation. Instead of descending on doubled rope as above, clip the rope through the anchor karabiner, tie the victim into the end of the rope and attach yourself to the other side with a descending device. Photo 78 shows the basic set-up. You will see that in this method the anchor acts as a sort of pulley but the lowering is still done by the rescuer. It is important that both rescuer and victim are connected as imbalances in weight may cause one to move down the cliff faster than the other.

I have also seen this system operated using an abseil device at the anchor point but feel that if anything should go wrong with the device, such as it jamming up, when you are halfway down you will be in a terrible predicament. It is better to avoid it happening in the first place.

The only advantage with this alternative method over the

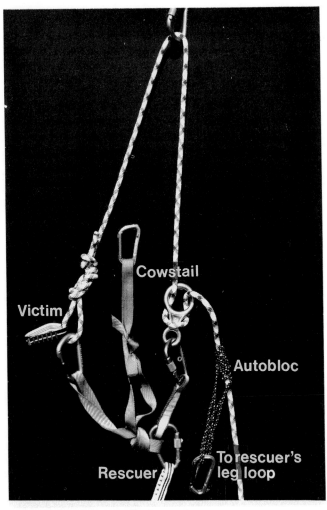

(78) Alternative method of assisted evacuation

standard one is that it is much easier and more immediate to adjust the positions of both the rescuer and the victim in relation to each other.

Direct Belays and Belaying Techniques

In traditional climbing procedure climbers safeguard each other with some kind of body belay or mechanical device. In doing so the belayer is placing him or herself between their companion and the anchor point to which both are ultimately attached. This can simply be referred to as an *indirect* belay or one in which the initial impact of a fall is taken by the belayer. When using a *direct* belay the load comes immediately on to the anchor. In the case of an indirect belay, some of the strain can be taken by the belayer's body thereby decreasing the load on the anchor points. Indeed, in cases where the anchors are poor or a little suspect, this is done deliberately. In the case of a direct belay however, the load will come immediately on to the anchor. It may be stating the obvious, but your anchors must be 100% sound.

Direct belays should always be treated with the utmost caution and you should always question your decision to use one. There is no doubt whatsoever though that in certain situations a direct belay is both quick, convenient and efficient to use. These situations occur most commonly in moderate terrain where there may be some risk of a fall but not enough to warrant a full blown belay and stance. They occur in winter climbing quite frequently and the technique is in common usage in Alpine regions where, combined with moving together techniques (see page 184), it forms the basis of all Alpine ropework.

Direct belays can take on many guises. They may be rock spikes or flakes, large boulders, trees, chocks wedged in a crack, pitons, slings around chockstones, snow or ice anchors – in fact almost any kind of anchor commonly used in climbing.

The techniques of using each anchor vary too. You may drape the rope directly around a spike or you may place a sling around it instead and clip the rope in with an Italian hitch. Whatever the anchor and method you decide to use *always* remember that the set up must be able to cope with the full weight of a fall and that if it fails you are powerless to halt the consequences.

USING THE ROPE DIRECTLY AROUND A ROCK OR TREE

After the soundness of the anchor the second most important consideration is to be sure that the rope will not slip off the anchor if you have to hold a fall. Sometimes the anchor may be quite shallow or rounded and not accommodate the rope effectively. The anchor, particularly if it is a spike or flake may also have sharp edges which abrade the rope and may even cause it to break when a load is applied. What is surprising to most people who use direct belays of this kind for the first time is the ease with which a fall, particularly that of a second, can be held. The amount of friction generated by a turn around even the smallest flake or spike can be impressive.

As a general rule in all direct belaying, the more rope you are able to have in contact with the anchor, the greater the friction will be. The greater the friction, the easier it is to hold a falling climber. It is important when belaying a second in this fashion that the rope is kept taut at all times and you should pay particular attention to the way in which the rope is taken in. Ensuring that you never let go of the controlling rope is crucial. To hold a fall more effectively grip the two ropes together with the hand that holds the live rope (Photo 79).

Unless you are able to arrange for a satisfactory upward pulling anchor, you should not use this particular method for belaying the leader. You can use direct belay techniques to belay a leader but only with upward pulling anchors and by connecting the rope to the anchor via a karabiner.

USING THE ROPE THROUGH A KARABINER

If you decide that you are going to use a sling around a spike or

(79) Direct belay around a spike

a nut in a crack or a thread anchor, or bolts, pegs or ice screws you will have to connect the rope to the anchor via a karabiner.

You will have to use some sort of friction device in order to hold a fall. This could be a belay plate, a figure of eight descendeur or an Italian hitch. If you decide to use a belay plate make sure that you can operate it correctly by standing behind the plate (see page 71). In practice the plate is awkward to use and requires an almost purpose made stance to operate it safely so an Italian hitch or a figure of eight may be preferable. It is possible to operate both the latter devices from in front of the anchor, which will in fact be found more convenient in the majority of cases.

The rope can be used directly through the karabiner without any friction device at all. It is essential to wear leather gloves if you want to give yourself any chance of being able to hold someone. In unpractised hands however this is not a terribly safe method and if for some reason your partner falls off and you are unable to hold the rope, the consequences may well be fatal. You will no doubt see it used on the mountains however and that is the main reason for mentioning it here. The only term I've ever come across for this method is the 'Australian glove belay'. It is possible to make it a little safer by putting a second turn around the karabiner. This unfortunately has a tendency to twist the ropes quite badly.

A further consideration worthy of a few words is the combination of a belay device, such as a plate or hitch attached directly to the belayer or even a body belay, but with the rope running through or around a direct belay. This allows the belayer to hold the rope more easily yet utilizes the speed of a direct belay. In most cases it would not be necessary for the belayer to anchor to the mountain. Indeed if that was necessary it would negate the advantages of the direct belay.

Moving Together

Moving together is the commonly used term for situations where two, or more, climbers are roped together for safety and moving up, down or across the mountain but do not go through the traditional sequence of making stances and climbing one at a time.

The technique is most often used in moderate terrain where there may be the potential of a serious slip or fall but in consideration of speed and efficiency of movement on the mountain it does not justify traditional belaying and climbing techniques. Such terrain includes easy but exposed scrambling, easy snow climbs and glacial travel. It is a tenuous form of safety that relies on good technique, quick reactions and an ability to handle ropes and equipment slickly.

It is a technique that is generally criticized in the UK for its apparent disregard of safety but one that is practised in Alpine regions more frequently than any other technique. In these pages I will try to dispel some of the myth but will make no attempt to denounce the serious implications of using it in the mountains.

MOVING TOGETHER – TWO ON THE ROPE

This is moving together in its simplest form. Two climbers of fairly equal ability and experience and moderate rock scrambling terrain such as might be found on an easy classic Alpine peak or the Cuillin on Skye.

The first decision that has to be made is how much rope to have between the two climbers. This can be a problem because too much rope out may lead to complications and inevitably, tangles and not enough rope to greatly reduced safety margins. Unfortunately there is no hard and fast rule that can be applied as each situation dictates a different course of action.

A good starting point, however, is to have about 10 m between each climber. The remainder of the rope can be shared equally between the two people or carried by one person. If the decision is for one person to carry it, it is as well to give it to the more experienced as he or she will be the one most likely to need it. This will be particularly true if route-finding is a problem or having just surmounted a short section of difficult climbing, one finds that to go on a further 7 m or so will lead to a safer stance and/or better anchor.

Photos 80a and b and 81 show a recommended way to shorten the rope by coiling it around the body. There are many ways of tying the rope off at the harness but, though not usually dogmatic in my approach to these things, I suggest that this is one of the simplest and most effective. It is also particularly easy to release more rope as it is required.

When coiling the rope around your shoulder you should try to make each coil about waist length. Anything shorter will have you walking round like Quasimodo all day and anything longer will make you angry as you'll be tripping over the loops. Please remember that it is important to tie the coils off for safety reasons. If you don't and you have to hold a falling climber the coils will tighten up around your body and probably strangle you.

Most of the time you will find it easier to move with a few coils in your hand (Photo 82a). Here again make the coils quite short so that there is little risk of tripping over them. Make sure that you take coils working from the thumb outwards. This will allow you to drop coils easily as and when they are required. Photo 82b shows a good way to lock off the coils. If you have to change the coils to the other hand you must turn the whole bunch around before doing so. As a general rule you should always try to carry the coils in the downhill hand. This means that if someone falls off below you the rope is not pulled across your body as the strain comes on to it.

Photo 82c shows another method of carrying coils. This is called 'lapping' the rope and though favoured by some climbers it is certainly not as popular nor is it as easy to hold a 'falling'

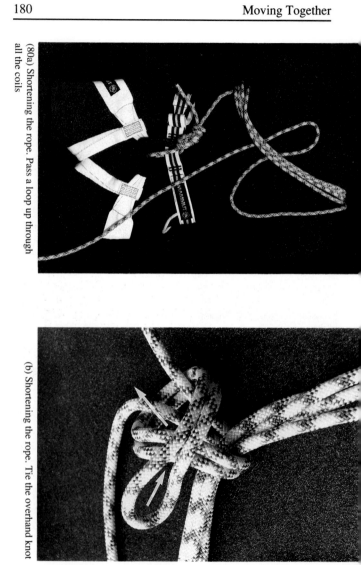

(80a) Shortening the rope. Pass a loop up through all the coils

(b) Shortening the rope. Tie the overhand knot

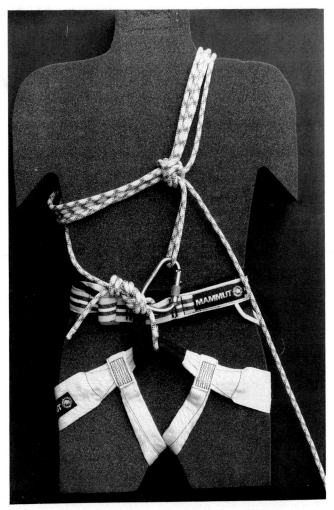

(81) Shortening the rope. The finished version

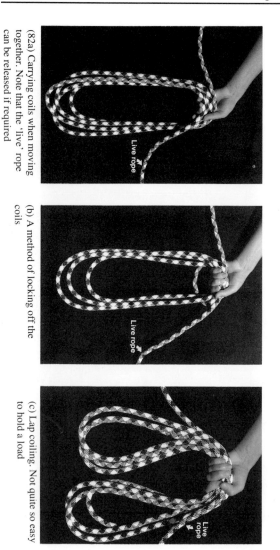

(82a) Carrying coils when moving together. Note that the 'live' rope can be released if required

(b) A method of locking off the coils

(c) Lap coiling. Not quite so easy to hold a load

climber.

On easy ground where it is possible to climb without using hands, it is as well to move quite close together – say 3-4 m apart – with the remainder of the rope carried by each climber. On slightly more difficult terrain or particularly on snow slopes you should only take coils on the rope that goes to the person below you. This affords a greater margin of safety when it comes to correcting a slip as the rope can be pulled tight immediately. There is no risk of them letting go of coils and thereby gaining speed and momentum in the fall. It goes without saying that the most experienced member of the party should be in the highest up the hill position. If for some reason this person slips you can only pray that they are able to stop themselves.

If the terrain requires the use of both hands you will most likely find it easier to move with the 10 m of rope out. In order to afford safety for both climbers the lead climber should put on running belays. These running belays may take the traditional form of a nut or a sling over a spike or a Friend or a piton. They could equally be the rope simply draped around a spike or a boulder or even just being on the opposite side of the ridge to your partner. These 'natural' running belays need to be treated with caution as sharp edges may cut the rope in the event of a fall. I recall a climb in New Zealand (not a recommended outing, I can tell you) where the rocks on the ridge were so sharp we moved together with the rope 'quadrupled' between us. If the lead climber continues to put on running belays in this way, he or she will soon run out and the person behind will be laden down with all the kit. So, from time to time you will need to meet up with your partner and either swap leads or swap equipment.

When you come across something difficult on the climb and you feel the need for greater security, it is a simple matter to arrange a more traditional belay. You may decide to use all of the rope or just a portion of it. Similarly you may decide to anchor yourself as in pitched climbing or use a direct belay which is probably more appropriate to the technique of moving together.

In either case it is quick to drop coils from your body to gain extra length. In some cases only one of the climbers need drop coils. It really depends on how much rope is required.

Direct belays (see page 174) play an important role in moving together techniques so it is well to practise until you are familiar with the different types of direct belay.

Please note that moving together does not afford the safety of traditional pitch climbing. One cannot hope to hold a serious leader fall or even, if they have the opportunity to gather momentum, a second falling for that matter. Safety lies in keeping the rope tight between each climber and being on the ball and quick enough to correct a slip before it turns into something a lot more serious.

MOVING TOGETHER – THREE ON THE ROPE

The techniques are essentially the same as two on a rope. It is probably advisable that the middle person ties on without taking any coils. Also you should consider carefully how you tie the rope into the harness. The easiest way is to tie a figure of eight or an Alpine butterfly knot and clip it to the harness via a screwgate karabiner. However, there are some harnesses that do not function correctly or safely if you do this. The Whillans harness is one such example. With this harness you must tie in to the loops as per the manufacturer's recommendation. To tie into the harness take the portion of rope that you want to tie into and thread it (it will be doubled) through the tie in loops and tie a bowline knot treating the doubled rope as one rope. The resulting knot is terribly bulky but it is really the safest way of tying in. Incidentally, there is nothing to stop you from tying the middle of the rope into all harnesses this way (Photo 83).

Tying on to the middle of the rope often presents problems for that person. He or she can literally be torn between two climbers. To avoid this occurring it is advisable to tie the figure of eight or the Alpine butterfly with a long loop and then to tie

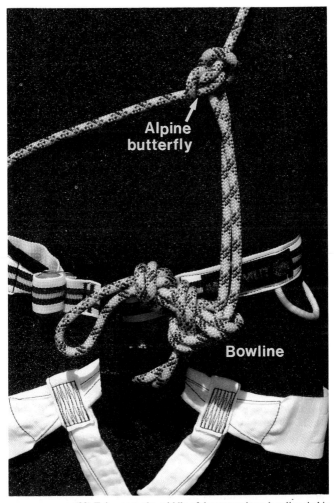

(83) Tying on to the middle of the rope using a bowline tied in
a loop of rope through the tie in loops of the harness

a figure of eight in the loop which is then clipped in to the harness (Photo 14). This then allows a certain amount of freedom of movement for the middle person. You should ensure that the distance between the harness and Alpine butterfly or figure of eight is such that it can never go out of arm's reach.

It is quite possible to have an infinite number of people on a rope thus, and keep on adding ropes and ropes, but sense and sensibility dictate that there must be a limit. I would venture to suggest that this be something like four or five to a rope on very easy ground and less as the terrain becomes more difficult. The exception to the rule is glacier travel, in which case the more the merrier for safety purposes. Glacier travel is dealt with under a separate heading for although it is still technically moving together, the specific techniques are a case apart.

LEADER BRINGING TWO CLIMBERS UP AT THE SAME TIME

This technique is used quite often in guiding or instructional situations and is a fairly quick way of mixing traditional pitch technique with moving together. It can be used effectively by a team of three climbers where movement up the climb would otherwise be a slow and tedious process. If used efficiently there is no reason why three shouldn't move almost as quickly as two. The lead climber should of course be experienced enough to be able to handle bringing two climbers up at the same time. Traditional anchoring methods are relevant but obviously one needs to consider the fact that you may have to hold both climbers at the same time, so make sure that anchors are good.

The method of belaying should also be given careful consideration. A body belay such as the waist or shoulder belay is not enough. It should be a belay plate or similar device or possibly an Italian hitch. Whatever system you decide to use the rope to each of the climbers you are safeguarding must operate independently of the other. An Italian hitch in both ropes together,

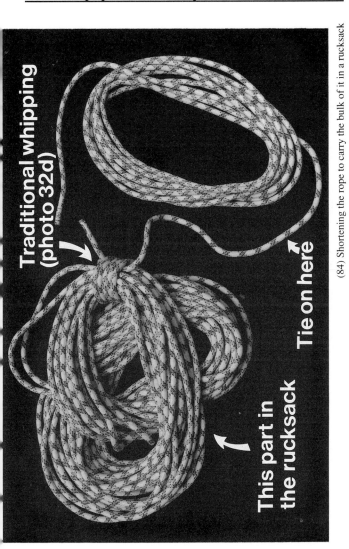

Traditional whipping
(photo 32d)

This part in
the rucksack

Tie on here

(84) Shortening the rope to carry the bulk of it in a rucksack

clipped into one krab will not work efficiently.

The two climbers, rather than climb side by side, should move about 5 m apart, one behind the other. They should be tied into clearly identifiable ropes so that the belayer is aware of who's doing what at any time. On difficult or serious terrain it may not be practical to bring both climbers up at the same time. An advantage of this system is that it is convenient to revert to traditional pitched climbing at any time and use the moving together technique on easier or less serious ground. When belaying the leader either of the 'seconds' may take on the task or both could belay the leader on their own ropes.

Other Methods of Shortening the Rope

In other situations, for example if you only want to safeguard a less experienced or more cautious companion over a short tricky section of a climb, it would be laborious and unnecessary to go through the previous procedure.

Photo 84 shows a method where only a part of the rope is used and the remainder stored in the rucksack. This will obviously cause problems if you discover that you need more rope than you have instantly available, so be sure that you have enough to hand. Never just 'stuff' the spare rope in your rucksack as I can guarantee you will snag it somehow and pull it all out of the pack.

There are a couple of other ways of tying off the rope as well as the one described, but so long as the rope is tied off neatly and securely it doesn't really matter how it's done.

Glacier Travel

Glacier travel is an important aspect of Alpine mountaineering. The most serious part of an Alpine climb is often the approach up a glacier or the descent at the end of the day. It is an aspect of mountaineering that is all too often taken lightly and without due regard to safety – until you fall into a crevasse – and then it becomes apparent that the words of caution were not spoken lightly.

Glaciers, like climbs, can be easy or complicated and difficult to negotiate. There is however no system of categorizing the difficulty of glacier travel, nor indeed would it be practical to do so. What one week may be a straightforward stroll, a week later could be a complicated mass of yawning crevasses and hungry crevasse tigers. It is not within the remit of this book to discuss the mountaineering skills of route-finding, suffice to say in these pages that glacier travel and its associated dangers should be treated with the utmost respect.

Before you decide on a method of roping up for glacier travel, it may be as well to consider the prerequisites. The rope is required for the safety of the party in negotiating crevassed areas where the dangers may not be visually apparent but may well result in a fall into a crevasse. In many cases a fall into a crevasse is only up to the chest level and extrication is a simple matter. If, however, you are crossing a large snow bridge and it collapses you may end up hanging well below the lip of the crevasse – maybe even dangling in space. You may also sustain an injury on the way down or be knocked unconscious. In just about every case you almost certainly lose contact with your companions on the surface. The rope must therefore be attached to the climber in such a way that it affords safety to someone falling into a crevasse *and* that it is possible for those who remain on the surface first to hold and later to secure and rescue any climber from a crevasse. There are numerous methods of tying on to the rope, some of which will be discussed here and others

(85) Every which way but loose! Glacier travel through complex terrain

that I propose to leave to self discovery.

To begin with let us consider the choice of harness. By far the most commonly used in mountaineering is the sit harness. Whilst such a harness is adequate for nearly all climbing scenarios, any of which might result in a fallen climber hanging free with a heavy rucksack on their back, it may cause the climber to tip upside down and even fall out of the harness. For this reason I recommend that you give careful thought to the type of harness used in Alpine mountaineering and if for you a full body harness is not a worthwhile buy, that you consider using a chest harness, improvised or otherwise, and connect it to the sit harness. There are a number of lightweight and efficient chest harnesses available and one such is shown in Photo 86b. A two-piece system such as this allows the climber the choice of sit or full body harness applicable to whatever they may be doing. The sequence of photographs shows a way to use the rope to connect the two together (Photos 86a and b).

Generally speaking you should move on a glacier with about 8-10 m of rope between each climber in much the same way as the moving together techniques already described (page 178). This allows a good margin of safety for holding a falling climber and also enough rope for exploratory probing. Anything more than this often leads to tangles and confusion and anything less lowers the safety margins considerably. It is, however, important to remember that unlike other methods of moving together, you must *not* at any time carry coils in the hand.

The basis of the safety system lies in keeping the rope tight between the climbers at all times. By allowing slack to develop you increase the length of any fall and decrease your chances of success in holding someone securely. The minimum safe number of climbers on a rope is obviously two. Obviously, the more climbers on the rope the greater the margins of safety and the greater the likelihood of stopping someone should they fall into a crevasse. The longest 'rope' of climbers I have ever seen was about 73 – it was difficult to keep count! This was on the Tour

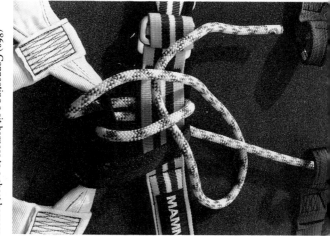

(86a) Connecting a sit harness to a chest harness

(b) The completed connection

Glacier in Chamonix.

Regardless of the number of climbers on the rope it is important to ensure that there is sufficient spare rope in the party to effect a rescue. This can be carried in coils around the body or in the rucksack or you might even have a complete spare rope in your pack.

In theory, the 'safest' position on the rope in glacier travel is in between two other climbers. Here you have a rope from both sides so the chances of being stopped before you fall too far are quite high – provided of course that your companions are alert. It is quite possible that you could spend a lifetime travelling over glaciers and not fall into anything serious that requires complex rescue procedures. But it is such an unknown quantity that it would be foolish to become complacent. At all times you must be 'on the ball' and ready to hold a fall.

ROPING-UP TECHNIQUES

Two on the Rope

For two climbers moving on a glacier you should rope-up, as I said before, about 8-10 m apart. Use the middle of the rope leaving on a 45 m rope, for example, about 18 m at either end. This spare rope is then coiled around the body in the way shown in Photos 80 and 81. The coils must be tied off in the manner illustrated. This method of tying on has the advantage that it creates a chest support which is particularly effective if the coils are reasonably snug around the shoulder. In the event of a fall, the initial impact is taken on the sit harness and the coils support the upper body.

You should always put a 'prusik' loop on the rope. I recommend that this be the longest of the loops that you have so that if you do fall down a crevasse you do at least have something that you can stand in immediately. You will find this important from the point of view of comfort. Whilst walking along the glacier the spare cord can be tucked in the pocket or tied loosely to the harness.

For reasons that will soon become apparent use a Klemheist knot and tie a figure of eight knot in the sling about halfway along. This is then used as a handle to assist with keeping the rope out from under your feet and more importantly to help hold a falling companion (page 203). The leading climber is the one at most risk of falling into a crevasse. But don't think that you're excused the pleasure just by being at the back! For the people behind the leader the Klemheist can be used as a handle to assist you with holding a fall and it is also a convenient knot to use when the time comes to secure the rope prior to rescuing a companion from a crevasse (see Crevasse Rescue page 201).

When moving over the glacier keep the rope taut at all times, particularly when there are route-finding difficulties and the leading climber is probing for hidden crevasses. If necessary, you should not hesitate to use a temporary belay of some kind (see page 103) to safeguard each other over difficult or danger-ous snow bridges.

Three or More on a Rope

I would venture to suggest that four climbers would be the maximum number that you should consider tying into one 45 m or 50 m length of rope. This allows for about 9 m of rope between each person and about 9 m spare at either end for effecting rescues. You may of course have a whole rope spare in a party of four climbers which can be used to work on a rescue. The people in the 'middle' of the rope could tie on in the manner recommended on page 184. Give careful consideration to whether or not these people should be tied into a full body harness, improvised or otherwise. My suggestion is that they should be, but, as there is much less chance of them falling a long way into a crevasse it is possible to get away with wearing a sit harness. It is, however such a simple matter to rig an improvised chest harness which will at least provide some support, that you may be foolhardy not to do so. Photo 87 shows a method of making

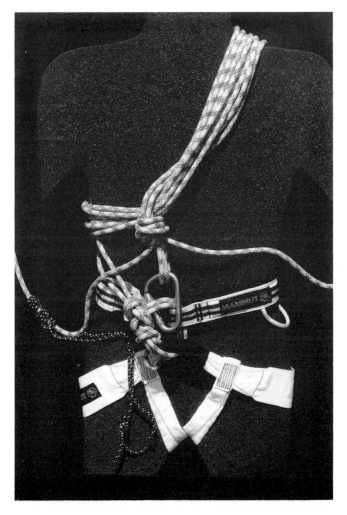

(87) Tying on to the middle of the rope using coils for chest support

an improvised chest harness from the rope. Each 'middle' person should put a prusik loop on the rope to the climber in front of them. This can then be used as a handle to assist with holding the person in front of you.

Do not become complacent with regard to safety. Just because there is safety in numbers, it doesn't mean you're exempt from the experience of falling into a crevasse. Keep the rope taut at all times and *don't* carry coils.

SAFETY WHEN NEGOTIATING DIFFICULTIES

Snow bridges

If you should come across a seemingly weak or a narrow snow bridge it is important that each climber be safeguarded across. It is not enough to casually stroll along and hope that nothing will happen. Often it may be safety enough that the person behind keeps the rope very tight and moves forward only as the one crossing the bridge needs rope. All other people on the rope should keep the rope tight and be similarly braced. Once one person is across this procedure can be repeated for the remainder of the party. Make sure though that you keep the party strung out and don't gather together in one spot. It has happened that parties have grouped together over a crevasse and the whole thing has collapsed depositing everyone in the hole.

If you feel the need for a more solid form of anchor you may choose to make one of the snow anchors described in the section on snow and ice anchors. It would be true to say however, that in the majority of cases keeping the rope tight is more than adequate.

Jumping a Crevasse

Jumping over crevasses, whilst testing your long jump skills, can be a dangerous thing to do. It is often necessary though, and you would be as well to bear a few things in mind. Firstly ensure that the person jumping has enough rope to make the distance! That sounds a bit obvious but I have witnessed a few occasions where there hasn't been enough rope and either the person jumping was pulled back into the crevasse or the next person on the rope had to make a hurried decision to jump. Make sure that you have as good a take off as possible and that the landing is fairly safe. Jumping downhill is the most risky because it is often difficult to control the momentum. If you have someone who is a little nervous about jumping you can wait for them to jump and, if you don't think that they are going to make it, assist them by pulling on the rope! It works, just so long as you don't pull before they jump.

You may decide that you need a more secure anchor and belay in which case use an appropriate system from the chapter on anchors on snow, rock and ice.

Crossing a Bergschrund

Depending on the size of the bergschrund you have to cross, it is likely that you will treat this aspect of mountaineering as a 'pitched' climb. You may not rig-up the anchors as you would do in a fully fledged pitch situation but you will certainly move one at a time.

In ascent, having chosen the crossing point, the leader will go across. He or she will be belayed by the next person along the rope. This could once more, be a simple matter of keeping the rope taut. In descent, again depending on the size of the beast, it is probably better to gather together at a convenient position above the bergschrund and rig up a belay. Try to make sure that you have a fairly comfortable stance. This may mean hacking out a large platform to stand on or if the climb you are on is fairly popular the stance will probably be large enough.

The leader or most experienced member of the party will probably go last. All other members may be lowered down or they may climb to safety. If there is room it is a good idea for all the party to spread out along the length of rope available and keep it taut to afford extra safety. The last person over the 'schrund' is protected by all the others keeping the rope respectably taut – though not so tight that you run the risk of pulling the person off. Should the leader discover that the bergschrund is straightforward enough to cross without resorting to belaying each member, the party can resume a moving together technique and treat the obstacle just like another crevasse.

Occasionally it will be necessary to abseil over a bergschrund. Try, if possible, to do this near to some rocks and you may be able to use a rock anchor. If there is no rock anchor available you will either have to abseil off a bollard – the most likely – or an ice screw or a retrievable T-axe. (See chapters Anchors on Snow and Ice and Other Useful Rope Tricks.)

At risk of repeating myself, I would like to reiterate the importance of good rope management and a sensible approach to glacier travel. Too often one is witness to sloppy technique and accidents, including deaths, that could so easily have been avoided.

Crevasse Rescue

'To come down a glacier without relaxing the essential precautions asks, in most cases, for a special and sustained effort of will. It is usually done in the afternoon; the party is tired; the snow is softening in the warm sun; the hard climb is over and everyone is relaxed; it is easy to be careless. This, above all, is the time when people fall into crevasses. It may sound strange but it happens again and again. The leader is sinking knee-deep into soft snow; the second man, hot and exhausted, full of the wish to be off the glacier as soon as possible, closes up to the leader; the third man is bored by walking alone and closes up to the second; their ropes trail behind them. Then someone goes through.'

From *On Climbing* by Sir Charles Evans, Museum Press, 1956.

Salutary words indeed, but so true.

This chapter deals with the techniques of getting out of a crevasse. Many of the techniques have already been discussed and it is simply a matter of putting them in context and discussing where and what will work best. As with all self-rescue situations, no two are ever the same. The circumstances are nearly always different; the time of day, the seriousness of the terrain, the abilities of individuals concerned and so it goes on. Armed with a repertoire of techniques however, the mountaineer can usually effect a rescue.

THE BASIC CREVASSE RESCUE

The most common 'fall' into a crevasse is going through up to the waist or chest at the worst. Extraction is largely a matter of self preservation. That is to say, as soon as you feel your feet kicking around in space and that void below you, some strange power takes over and you're no sooner in than you're out. With a little help from your friends of course.

The serious problems begin when you are below ground level. Provided that your partner or partners have been doing their job well and the rope has been kept tight, you shouldn't fall too far into the crevasse. However, as soon as you go below ground level the rope will cut into the snow on the edge of the crevasse and this will give most of the problems.

To stop someone who is falling into a crevasse, the first thing you must do is fall to the ground and try to dig your feet in. There will probably be a few micro-seconds when you think you're not going to be able to hold but it is usually surprisingly easy, particularly if the rope cuts deep into the edge and creates a lot of friction. If you are the one who has fallen in and are literally only just below the surface, you may be able to get out with a struggle and a fair amount of tugging from your partners. If despite all the tugging and heaving and pushing, the rope remains stuck fast and you don't pop out, you must adopt a slightly more scientific approach. The climber, on the surface may decide to secure you to an anchor and come to the edge to help you. If there are three or more climbers on the rope, you can be held by the second person along while a third comes to your aid. Whoever it is that goes to the edge, they must make sure that they have some kind of protection just in case they fall through too. This will mean rigging an anchor for the second person, and then the third can go to the edge with the protection of a prusik loop on the loaded rope. This can be moved along as the climber approaches the edge.

When the rescuer gets to the edge the first thing to do is to put something, such as a spare ice axe, ski poles or rucksack, under the rope to try to prevent it from cutting deeper into the crevasse edge. After that it is possible to cut away a little of the edge in order to reveal the buried rope. *Take care* when hacking the snow away from around the loaded rope because the slightest touch may well be enough to cut it. Remember, a loaded rope cuts very easily. You should have a very good chance of getting out once all that has been done, without having to resort to complicated pulley systems and hoists.

The 'Real' Thing!

If despite careful ropework or because of a lack of attention, a climber disappears well below the surface, you will have something more serious to deal with. One of the problems confronting you from the outset will be the lack of ability to communicate between surface and crevasse and this will frustrate attempts at rescue. It is important that you establish with all of the party, before you go out in the mountains, exactly what will happen if one of the group falls deeply into a crevasse. This will speed up the rescue procedure because at least everyone has an idea of what is going on, including, most importantly, the person down the crevasse.

As a general rule, once someone has fallen into a crevasse the person on the surface should rig up an anchor and escape from the system. Meanwhile the person in the crevasse should, provided they are able, make sure that they have their prusiks on the rope. They will almost certainly have one, but may not have the other on so do that immediately. At the same time try to take stock of the situation and decide the best way to get out of the hole.

When escaping from the system on the surface, life is made much more straightforward by having a prusik loop already on the rope. If you use, as suggested in the previous chapter, a Klemheist in the long prusik loop, it is a simple matter to convert it to a French prusik autobloc. Photos 88, 89 and 90 show the sequence of escaping from the system 'crevasse rescue' style. The escape can be effected in much the same way as it is done on a rock climb. Refer to the appropriate pages for more detail. The procedure is as follows.

Take the strain of the fallen person by immediately dropping to the ground and digging your feet in. Once you have stopped sliding and your partner falling you have to try to get an anchor in. This could be any of the snow anchors described in the chapter on snow, rock and ice anchors, but remember that the snow may be very soft and unpredictable.

If there are more than two of you on the rope, it is preferable to get someone behind you to rig the anchor. You would do well not to underestimate the difficulty of holding someone's weight while trying to arrange an anchor. Having rigged the anchor, you must then convert the Klemheist to a French prusik, as in Photo 88 and clip it into the anchor. Having done that move forward gradually to take all the weight off yourself and transfer it to the anchor. That done you can untie all the coils from around you and untie completely. Make sure that you tie the rope into the anchor with a separate krab before doing anything else. This is your safety back-up in the event that the autobloc fails (Photo 90).

As soon as you have escaped from the system you must try to establish contact with the person down the crevasse. To do this you will need to go to the edge of the crevasse. It would be sensible to approach the edge of the crevasse very cautiously and

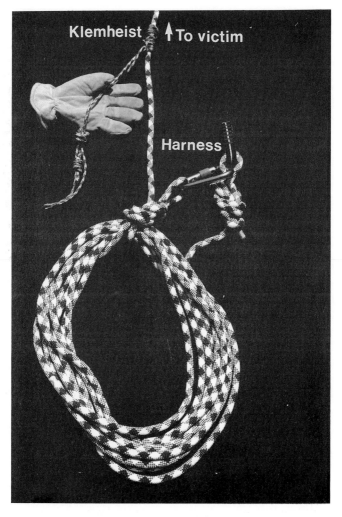

(88) Escaping the system during crevasse rescue – stage one

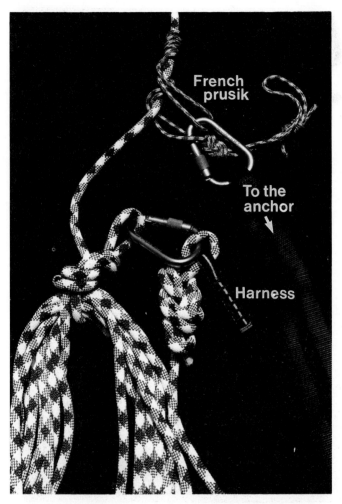

(89) Having rigged your anchor, convert the Klemheist to a French prusik and clip it to the anchor – stage two

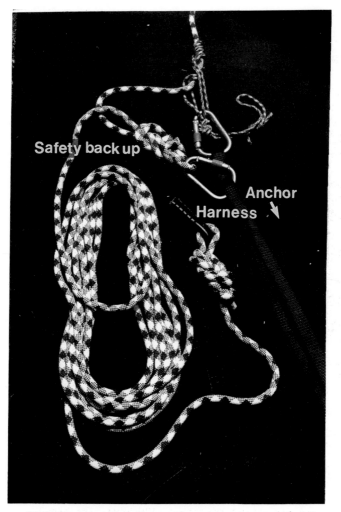

(90) The final stage. The escape complete you can now rescue the victim

on hands and knees with a prusik loop on the load rope or some other safety device attached to the anchor. This of course could be a spare rope or the remaining rope that was coiled around your shoulder. Once on the edge, put some padding or something under the rope to prevent it cutting any deeper into the crevasse edge.

When you have established communication you can decide, between the two of you, on the best course of action. It may be that the person down the crevasse decides to prusik out. If so, you will need to sort out the edge of the crevasse so that it is easier for the crevasse bound climber to get out. This will certainly involve plenty of hacking away at the edge and a deluge of snow down onto the victim. If you are unable to clear away the snow from around the loaded rope the best thing to do is to cut a box-shaped slot just to the side of where the rope has cut in. You could then drop a spare bit of rope down this to help the victim get over the very awkward final edge. This can be used to pull the victim out or for them to transfer to when they arrive near the top.

If you are the person that has to prusik out you will find it easier to do so without a rucksack on. As you begin to ascend you will notice that a loop of slack rope develops. This loop will get longer the higher you go. As soon as you can identify this loop, take off your rucksack and clip it into the loop so that it hangs below you. If you have skis on you can dangle them from this loop too. Be careful not to drop any equipment!

The party may decide that an assisted hoist (page 154) is the answer to the problems. In which case set the ropes up for the hoist in the way illustrated in Photo 69 but you need not put on the belay plate of course. The biggest problem you will encounter here is getting the hoisting loop down to the victim. Once achieved however, extraction is a simple matter – well, fairly simple. Never discount the possibility that the person who has fallen down the hole might be able to walk out out along a snow bridge if lowered down a short distance.

Dealing with Problems

The most likely problem to occur is that the rope will have cut so deeply into the edge of the crevasse that it is completely jammed. In this event you will be unable to use it to aid the rescue. If the victim decides to prusik out, he or she should do so on this rope up to the point that it disappears into the edge. Meanwhile the people on the surface should rig up a second rope for the victim to transfer to for the final stage out.

If you have to do a hoist, assisted or otherwise, a slightly different approach to that previously described is required. Escape as illustrated in Photos 88-90 and go to the edge to cut a box shaped slot just to the side of the jammed rope. Make sure that you arrange something to prevent the rope from cutting deeper into the edge. Go back to the anchor and fix a second figure of eight knot in the rope and clip it into the anchor. If you have a spare sling then use this as it will become much less complicated around the anchor attachment (Photo 91). To all intents and purposes, the rope that originally held the victim becomes redundant, although at this stage their weight is still hanging on it.

Using the rope from the second figure of eight knot that you tied, drop a loop with a pulley attached, down to the victim. This is then clipped into the victim's harness at a secure place – preferably the central loop. If for some reason this loop is not long enough to reach the victim, it can be extended with a sling. The slack end of the rope is passed through an Alpine clutch or through a karabiner and pulley with a French prusik autobloc. On this rope and between the autobloc and the victim put on a short prusik loop. Take the rope from the other side of the autobloc and clip it to this prusik (Photo 90). By pulling on the rope indicated in the photo you should be able to hoist your victim. The victim can actually help a little by pulling on the rope that is attached to the second figure of eight knot that you tied earlier on. Once the load comes off the original holding rope a third person could, if desired, undo the figure of eight back-up, convert it to an Italian

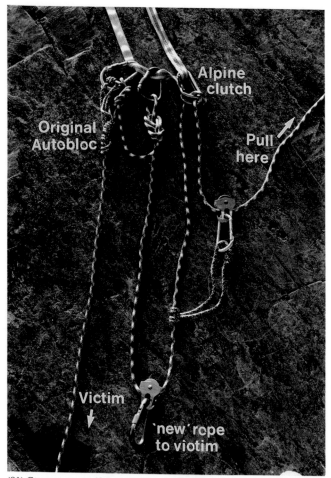

(91) Crevasse rescue if the main rope is jammed in the edge of the crevasse

hitch and take in the rope as the victim gains height.

Unconscious Victim

If the person who falls down the crevasse is injured or has been knocked unconscious, you will have very different problems to solve. Without doubt, the first thing to do is to go down to the victim and take stock of the situation. It may be necessary to administer First Aid. You must make sure that the anchor you have placed is strong enough to take the weight of two people. Invariably this will mean backing the original up with a second anchor or creating a new one just for the rescuer.

You will then probably have to hoist the victim to the surface. This in itself is a difficult and onerous task and not one to be undertaken lightly. It is tempting to say glibly here that you should go to the surface and rig up an unassisted hoist as illustrated in Photo 72 but in truth if you are on your own you have very little hope of being able to pull an unconscious victim to the surface. It is difficult enough even with two or three people. There is, however enough information in these chapters to give you a chance of rescuing an unconscious person but don't expect to be able to do it without some practice first – and certainly don't expect it to be easy.

Remember that small pulleys – such as those manufactured by Petzl – reduce friction. If none are available use double krabs to reduce the angle of the turn at each moving part of the system.

Hints on Practising Crevasse Rescue

Many people practise the techniques of crevasse extraction on a dry glacier i.e. one that is bare ice and where all the crevasses are visible. This is quite a good starting point to pick up the basics but it is not terribly realistic. It is much better to go to some real crevasses on a snow covered glacier to practise. You should be able to make everything perfectly safe by having back-up anchors for everything so that if someone fails to hold a falling

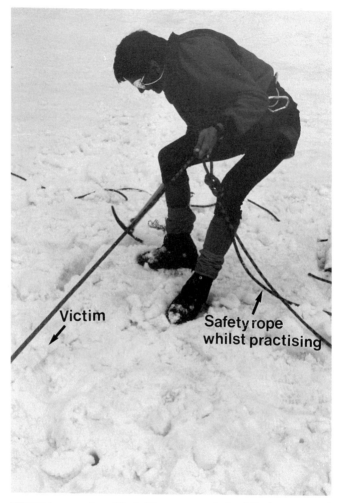

Victim

Safety rope
whilst practising

(92) Making an anchor whilst holding someone who has fallen in a crevasse.
In this case a T–axe is used

(93) Crossing a narrow snow bridge. The rope is taut in both directions

climber at least they are not all going to fall in.

I would suggest this as a worthwhile exercise as it gives you a more realistic idea of what to expect and, in my experience, makes you aware of the importance of not being too relaxed on a glacier. You need not even go to a glacier to practise. Small cornices or other features in the British hills in winter provide a similar formation to a crevasse. Please make sure that the 'run out' is perfectly safe – the top of Number 5 Gully on Ben Nevis would certainly not be ideal!

Other Useful Rope 'Tricks'

In this final chapter I propose to discuss a few techniques that didn't seem to fit in under any other headings but are, nevertheless, appropriate to a rope techniques book. The first two techniques are often labelled as pretty fancy tricks for instructors and guides only but this needn't be the case at all. Admittedly, they have limited use and sometimes don't work. Nonetheless, if they are set up correctly and with some thought, there will be occasions when you might find them useful.

RETRIEVABLE ICE SCREW

This trick will only work reliably with tubular screw in/screw out ice screws. The ice screw must not be too long and you must also make sure that the cord used to activate the retrieval is long enough to unscrew the ice screw completely. Photo 94 show the set-up in the ice ready for abseiling and the method for setting it up. The Penberthy knot must be attached to the rope that you are going to pull. If, therefore, you are abseiling on two ropes joined put the Penberthy just above the joining knot. The cord that initiates the turning of the screw must always be attached to the left hand rope. If it is attached to the right it will only tighten the screw into the ice! You could arrange the connection of ice screw to rope by using a piece of cord or tape and tying it into an overhand loop in the abseil rope. This works just as well as the method illustrated. When you put in the ice screw it is worthwhile unscrewing it and screwing it back in a couple of times to ensure that it will unscrew easily. This is particularly necessary if it is many degrees below freezing as the screw could freeze in tighter whilst you are abseiling.

RETRIEVABLE ICE AXE

A similar sort of gimmick to the retrievable ice screw but

Penberthy

(94) Retrievable ice screw

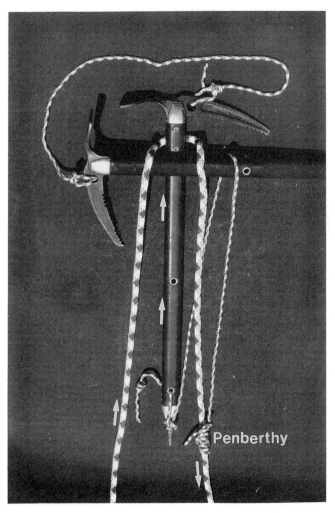

(95) Retrievable T-axe

nonetheless one that I know has been put to good use on a number of occasions, particularly abseiling over bergschrunds. Photo 95 shows the method for setting it up.

There are some important considerations to take into account. Firstly, the snow that you set the anchor up in must be fairly solid and reliable. When you are arranging the T-axe in the slot make sure that the vertical axe will run smoothly up and down the hole. The slot that you cut for the rope to run through should be a little wider than what you would cut for a normal T-axe anchor. This is to allow the rope to run more smoothly. Make sure that the cord that you use for the Penberthy knot at one end and the attachment to the spike of the vertical axe at the other, is quite long. The vertical axe must be pulled completely clear of the snow before the connection to the horizontal axe comes tight. Stand very well clear of the rope when you do retrieve the equipment! When pulling try to get the vertical axe out in one movement and keep up the momentum so that it pulls the horizontal one out with it.

TENSIONING ROPES FOR TYROLEANS AND OTHER AERIAL ROPEWAYS

There are probably few occasions in day to day climbing when you will need to tension ropes. However, if you are involved in taking people – youngsters or adults – into the outdoors, you will probably find yourself setting up death slides, Postman's Walks, Tyroleans and a whole manner of ropeway adventures.

The first such adventure I had was on my introduction to Rock climbing course run by Pete Crew and Al Harris from Wendy's Cafe in Llanberis. We had gone to Gogarth for the day climbing and having just endured a Harris boulder trundling session, whilst I was still at water level, we wandered over to Wen Zawn. Within a short space of time two ropes, knotted together were stretched across the Zawn from the top of Wen crack to the promontory down below. The knot was almost

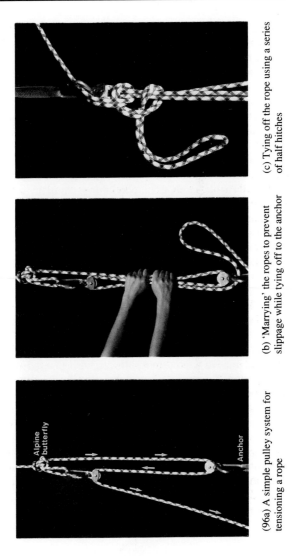

(96a) A simple pulley system for tensioning a rope

(b) 'Marrying' the ropes to prevent slippage while tying off to the anchor

(c) Tying off the rope using a series of half hitches

exactly halfway along. My only recollection of this adventure is of desperately trying to get past the knot without falling into the sea which was swirling and splashing and roaring what felt like thousands of feet below me. I've never done that tyrolean since!

One of the problems with setting up such a system with climbing ropes is that in order to get a good slide and the right amount of tightness in the rope, it is necessary to tension the ropes until all the stretch has been taken out. The strength of a climbing rope lies in its ability to absorb the shock of a falling climber. Taking all of the stretch out of the rope before you subject it to a load is putting the strain on it when it is at its weakest. This is surely not a good thing. On many occasions I have witnessed teams of ten or more people heaving on a climbing rope to get it guitar string tight and then bouncing about, see-sawing back and forth and generally subjecting it to forces that surely one day will cause their demise.

If you are involved in such activities on a regular basis you would be advised to buy a low- or non-stretch abseil rope specifically for such adventures. It is not then necessary to tension the ropes to near breaking point before you can use them. In fact it only requires a couple of people to set up. Not only that but the ropes themselves are much more durable.

Photos 96a, b and c show a tensioning system applicable to all aerial ropeways. Note that pulleys have been used at each turn in the rope. Every time you put a turn in the rope you are weakening it to a certain extent – the tighter the turn the weaker the rope. By putting pulleys at each turn the diameter of turn is much less and therefore weakens the system less. Once you have the right amount of tension in the rope and you want to secure it, get someone to hold the ropes as illustrated in Photo 96b. This is called 'marrying the ropes' and is a simple and effective way to ensure that you don't let any of the rope slip back through whilst tying it off. From time to time you will need to retension the ropes to keep them at the desired level of tightness. This is a simple matter. The tie off at the anchor can easily be undone even when under load.

Glossary of terms used in the text

Anchor
Point of security on a cliff. Can be anything from natural chockstones to Friends. To secure oneself to the crag or mountain.

Assisted Evacuation
Rescuer evacuates a victim who is incapacitated and unable to help in any useful way.

Assisted Hoist
Victim helps the rescuer to pull him/herself up the cliff.

Autobloc
A device that will lock around a rope and prevent slippage when a load is applied to the rope in a particular direction. It must also be capable of releasing itself when the rope is pulled the opposite way.

Belaying
The way in which a climber's rope is safeguarded whilst he or she is climbing. For example a belay plate or an Italian hitch.

Central Loop
The loop that is formed by the climbing rope when it is tied into a harness.

Dead Rope or Slack Rope
Any rope that does not have a climber directly on the end of it.

Doubled Snaplinks
Two snaplinks clipped in with the gates on opposite sides used for safety instead of a screwgate karabiner.

Escape from the System
    The technique of releasing oneself from the belay system and end of rope whilst ensuring the safety of the climber you are responsible for.

Hanging Hoist
    The technique of relieving the the weight from the end of the rope whilst someone is hanging on it.

In Situ
    Abbreviation for in situation i.e. gear that is already in place.

Jumaring
    Ascending a fixed rope using mechanical devices.

Load or Live Rope
    Any rope that has a climber directly on the end of it.

Multiple Anchors
    More than one anchor point.

Passing a Knot
    The technique of passing the join of two ropes through an abseiling or lowering device.

'Prusik'
    Any knot that will grip on to a thicker rope when a load is applied.

Prusiking
    Ascending a fixed rope with any kind of 'prusik' knot.

Safety Back-Up
    A back-up system should the main system fail.

Stance
A ledge or place where one anchors oneself to belay a climbing companion.

Tail end
The rope left over after tying a knot in the end of a rope.

Tie on loops
The loops of a harness through which the manufacturer recommends the rope to be threaded to tie into the harness.

Tying Off
The technique of securing a rope that is part of a belaying, abseiling or lowering system. It is also the method used to attach to pitons, both ice and rock, that haven't been inserted right up to the hilt.

Tying On
Fixing a climbing rope to a harness. Also used with reference to securing a climber to an anchor or anchor points.

Unassisted Hoist
The situation in which the rescuer hoists a victim who is incapacitated and unable to help in any useful way.

222

Index

Figures in *italics* refer to diagrams or illustrations